Listening to Young Writers

Listening to Young Writers

Developing Writing Competency through
Conversation, Engagement, and Assessment

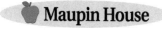 Maupin House

Listening to Young Writers: Developing Writing Competency through Conversation, Engagement, and Assessment
By Melissa Hare Landa

Cover design: MyJive, Inc.
Cover photography: Melissa Hare Landa
Author photo: Geoffrey T. Chesman
Book design: Mickey Cuthbertson

Library of Congress Cataloging-in-Publication Data
Landa, Melissa Hare.
Listening to young writers : developing writing competency through conversation, engagement, and assessment / Melissa Hare Landa.
    p. cm.
Includes bibliographical references.
ISBN 0-929895-81-9
1. English language—Composition and exercises—Study and teaching (Primary) 2. Language arts (Primary) 3. Language experience approach in education. I. Title.
LB1528.L26 2005
372.62'3—dc22   2005006381

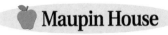

Maupin House publishes professional resources for K-12 educators. Contact us for tailored, in-school training or to schedule an author for a workshop or conference. Visit www.maupinhouse.com for free lesson plan downloads.

Maupin House Publishing, Inc.
800-524-0634
352-378-5588
www.maupinhouse.com

10 9 8 7 6 5 4 3 2 1

To my beloved children,
Shari and Adam.

And to

Joanne Busalacchi,
A gifted educator and a dear friend.

Contents

List of Charts

Acknowledgments

This book is a labor of love—love for children and appreciation for the chance they give all of us to listen and learn. I began this project five years ago, working in a remarkable school, under the guidance of an inspirational educator. Joanne Busalacchi nurtured my growth as a teacher in an environment that honored children and families. Her relentless vision of "children first" inspired me to develop the foundational ideas for this book and to pursue those ideas no matter how challenging that work could be. My thanks to Joanne are immeasurable.

Throughout this endeavor, I sought help and expertise from some remarkable educators and wonderful friends, to whom I feel gratitude. Charlotte Montgomery invited me to share my work with other teachers in the earliest days of this project and never tired of answering questions, offering guidance, and sharing her knowledge of early literacy. Floyd Starnes provided endless encouragement, support, and love, shared his expertise on second language acquisition, and offered invaluable feedback on my manuscript. Phyllis Kaufman shared her insights and encouraged me when I felt unsure. And Dr. Marci Fineman gave me opportunities to explore many of the ideas in this book and generously shared her thoughts with me during our many wonderful conversations. I would also like to mention Arturo Flores, who offered humor and encouragement during many months of writing, who inspired me with stories from his childhood about the plight of migrant farm workers, and who accompanied me when I took my work to Mexico.

I am also deeply indebted to Shelley Harwayne, whose work and wisdom have guided me and inspired me from the earliest days of my career, and who generously took time to read my manuscript. I also offer my thanks to my advisor, Dr. John O'Flahavan, and to my professor, Dr. Jeremy Price of the University of Maryland, and to Dr. Jerry Weast, superintendent of Montgomery County Public Schools.

I also owe thanks to the many talented teachers who shared their insights and who opened their classrooms to me. In particular, I thank Jane Patrick, Chris Manzone, Jennifer Williams, Bonnie Whitenight, Sarabeth Weiss, Susan Trella, Gabrielle Schechter, Wendy Gill, Pat Garwacki, and Annie

Moore. And thanks to Maria Garcia and Peggy Salazar for helping me contact many of my former students.

I also wish to thank my friends and trusted confidants, who supported me during the duration of this project, as well as for many years before, offering their encouragement, humor, patience, and love: Ruth Yodaiken, Sherrie Skipper, Wendy Berman, Floyd Starnes, Ellen Kaminow, Kasia Stanislawek, Heidi Dubin, Diana Friedman, and Kathy Mattimore. And my appreciation and love to all my wonderful students, who shared their thoughts and feelings with me in our classroom communities, where we learned and grew together.

Finally, my heartfelt thanks go to my family. To my mother, Isadora Hare, who taught me to have compassion, to work hard, to believe in myself, and to live with conviction; who guides me through the most challenging moments of life when I feel like giving up, and who tirelessly read and edited every version of this book. To my father, Philip Hare, who, since I was a child in South Africa, taught me about social justice, the immorality of poverty and racism, the importance of having a generous spirit and a strong sense of identity, and whose pride in me encourages me to pursue my dreams. To my sister, Rachel, who enriches my life in too many ways to mention, who was my first student, and who helped me begin the writing of this book. To my brother, Neil, who showed me that writing a book is, indeed, possible, and who generously offered his love and encouragement as I followed his lead. To my brother, Josh, who provides an example of hard work and dedication to one's profession and who offered calm during difficult moments of this project. To Lee and Kate, who never tired of listening to updates of this book, and to all the Hare and Landa families for their support.

And, I give special thanks and my love to my children, Shari and Adam, who are a constant source of delight and wonder to me (Yes, Mommy is finally done with the book!). And to my husband, Heinan, for encouraging my efforts, for his faith in me, and for being a wonderful father, giving our children many exciting adventures during the months and years that I sat and wrote this book.

Introduction

As teachers, we know that learning to write develops over time. We know that children have an inherent desire to "make their mark" as toddlers, using whatever surface they can find. We are aware that children learn the foundations of language by talking, first at home and then at school.

Some children bring to school large English vocabularies and the self-confidence that motivates them to speak and write, reflecting the benefits of years of conversation with attentive parents. Increasingly, however, many of our youngest students enter school with minimal experience with speaking English and in need of specialized instruction. Nearly nine million children between the ages of 5 and 17 living in the U.S. speak a language other than English, and 2.6 million of these children speak English with difficulty (Hodgkinson, 2003). Other youngsters from low-income homes who qualify for Head Start and Title I programs may or may not speak English but have limited early literacy experiences valued by schools.

As a teacher for 16 years—for most of that time at a school where over 75% of the children receive free or reduced lunch and where half the students are English Language Learners (ELL)—I have witnessed the challenges of poverty, language barriers, and illiteracy. As a Head Start teacher, I remember visiting my students' homes before the school year began. I remember seeing children in homes where sofas were their beds, which they shared with a sibling, and where empty refrigerator boxes served as containers for clothes.

Too often, teachers may write off these "Title I" children early. After all, they tend not to test well since the tools we have for assessing them focus on what they *do not* know, instead of measuring how far they have come. Yet they bring rich and complex life experiences to the classroom—separations from family members, the challenges of learning a new language, and other personal struggles. As a teacher, I learned that if I listened to them, acknowledged and embraced their life experiences, I could show them that they had valuable and important things about which to write.

Any child—regardless of the level of writing ability when he enters school—can progress and move towards becoming a capable writer. Briefly, that is the viewpoint of *Listening to Young Writers.* This book is about giving teachers instructional tools to move every child to writing competency—especially English Language Learners and children from low-income homes.

Consider second grader Antonio's writing below:

> When I came on the plane from Guatemala I was 3 years old. They didn't accept me at school because it was full. Then I started school when I was 4 and I was very happy. Then I talked English and my mom was happy. I learned from listening to my teacher and my friends. I was quiet but then I knew how to speak a little English. I was happy that I could show my family. If a person talks to us we won't understand the language if we don't know English. But now I understand what they are saying to me.

And first grader Rosa:

> My brother Enrique is coming to Maryland and I am so happy. He is bigger than me. I love him. He lives in Guatemala with my two sisters and my other brother. He talks in Spanish. He goes to school. I will show him to speak in English and write in English too. I will play with him. We will have fun.

To teach young children to write, we must listen and embrace the experiences they bring into our classroom, build on those experiences, and challenge any presumption that a child's formative experiences are not relevant to education. If we value and respect our students, we can use any experience they share with us as a seed for their learning.

Instead of viewing these children as "disadvantaged" and lowering our expectations, we should hold them up as examples of courage and resiliency and expect those qualities to lead them to academic success. Instead of defining immigrant children as "academically deficient," we can view them as world travelers and experts on their home cultures. We should also be awed by their budding bilingualism.

Children from low-income homes and children of immigrants, who may also live in poverty, straddle at least two cultures every day. This feat is impressive for anyone, let alone a child. As teachers, we must be cultural ambassadors to these students and find ways to make academic learning connect to their life experiences. As we do, they will learn not only how to write but the value of writing. By teaching them to write, we will help them and their families to prosper in American schools, jobs, business, and government.

The time we have with our students is a precious opportunity to show them that we expect them to succeed. We have the opportunity to give **all** our children six hours a day of achievement, success, and a sense of accomplishment. With skillful and strategic intervention, we can give all children the academic tools they need to feel empowered and to become competent writers.

Listening to Young Writers presents an organized and comprehensive approach to pre-K through second grade writing education that can be applied to a single primary class or to all primary classrooms in your school. All young writers profit from using this approach. It is especially useful for Title I schools or in schools with high ELL (English Language Learner) populations.

Listening to Young Writers helps us, as teachers, move every child along the continuum of writing development. The book offers strategies that help create a classroom environment that supports young writers, monitor writing behavior, assess student writing, identify "next-step" instructional goals, and implement the instructional strategies.

This resource helps you answer four questions critical to teach the youngest writers successfully:

- What are the children able to do?
- How can we be sure that we are not discouraging or overwhelming them?
- How can we make instruction relevant and meaningful for them?
- How can we help young writers attain the writing goals that have been identified?

Answering Those Questions

Since the youngest children learn to write by talking, Chapter 1 helps you set up a conversation-rich classroom, creating a writer-friendly atmosphere that validates the experiences of every child. This, in turn, builds self-esteem and a sense of trust that is necessary for the youngest writers.

Several informal and formal tools in Chapter 2 help you with the assessment of the writing competency and status of the young writers. A guide to assessing writing behavior provides a lens through which children's behavior can be observed as they sit in front of a blank piece of paper, with suggestions for redirecting problematic writing habits. This chapter also explains the value of a primary grade writing prompt to the overall writing program, with guidelines for administering and scoring the prompts.

Specific writing assessment rubrics developed to assess individual writing pieces are then explained, with a three-point writing rubric tailored specifically for emergent writers and two five-point rubrics that assess the use of writing craft and convention skills in developing writers.

Chapter 3 addresses the question, "How can we be sure that we are not discouraging or overwhelming students?" by showing teachers how to organize writing goals based on five basic characteristics of good writing. The goals are organized into an A, E, I, O, U system that makes sense for the youngest writers and helps you track progress easily. The chapter details how to set individualized goals for each child, based on this system. It also explains the importance of sharing just a few specific writing goals at a time and the wisdom of refraining from sharing abstract rubrics that focus on a young writer's deficiencies instead of his accomplishments.

The instructional strategies outlined in Chapter 4 answer another key question: "How can we make instruction meaningful and relevant to young writers?" The strategies provide a valuable instructional toolkit that supports the primary writing community.

The final question, "How can we help young writers attain the writing goals that have been identified?" is answered in Chapter 5, with specific mini-lessons that are correlated with the writing goals described in Chapter 2, and which serve as models as you develop your own "next-level" lessons.

Throughout, you will find specific information that will help you address the particular needs of children for whom English is a second language. Because ELL children learn to speak and write English at the same time, I explain the process of second language acquisition. You will see how each aspect of writing instruction parallels this process and, therefore, supports children who are learning to speak English.

Of course, it is important to teach systematically the fundamental structural skills that are required to write well in English. However, it is not our only job. We must also remember that children write because they want to. Their **desire** to express themselves launches, guides, and motivates them to learn those skills and continually brings them back to write again and again. Our task, therefore, is to nurture that desire and to make explicit the powerful place writing can hold in their lives and in our literate society.

When systematic teaching blends with sensitive and artful teaching, children learn that we write from our hearts as well as our minds, and in turn, they learn the power of the written word.

All children can discover the writers within them, not in spite of their lives but because of them. With this in mind, I offer this book to teachers, administrators, and student teachers, inviting all to join the privileged ranks of writing mentors for America's youngest writers.

Creating a Writer-Friendly Classroom

C hildren come to school from every type of background and home situation, bringing with them a diverse range of experiences and abilities. We as teachers have the power to create a supportive classroom environment that is rich in oral language, one that accurately assesses the abilities of children, monitors their progress, and empowers all students with the academic tools and self-confidence they need to become competent writers

The successful classroom that supports young writers:

- Allows questions that lead young students to explore thoughts, perceptions, and feelings;
- Confirms for children that their experiences are significant and meaningful and that others want to hear what they have to say;
- Helps children understand that the issues in their lives are reflected in books, and, therefore, books are relevant to them;
- Supports the development of speaking skills and active-listening skills;
- Shows children that their ideas, feelings, and experiences expressed orally can be transposed to the written word;
- Teaches children how to think like writers;
- Provides the teacher an opportunity to learn about each student, including aspects of the students' home life and home culture; and
- Creates opportunities for the students to learn about, and from, each other.

Writing Begins with Conversation

My approach to teaching writing to very young children presumes an inextricable connection between eliciting the motivating, creative aspects of writing and teaching the conventions of English.

By the time children enter kindergarten, some have already had years of practice with scribbling and improvised writing. Others respond eagerly to their first experiences with pencil and paper. How those first efforts are received by the teacher in large part determines how they will learn how to express themselves in writing.

The first step in writing for young children is speaking. They must process their thoughts aloud before they know what they are thinking, and then they become invested in their topics. Conversation is a helpful pre-writing activity for any writer, but it is by far the most effective pre-writing strategy for very young writers.

Without the opportunity to think aloud before they begin to write, children may not know *how* to begin to write about their topic even if it is meaningful for them. They might also create a list of ideas without understanding how to develop any of them.

Traditionally, teachers place a blank piece of paper in front of each student and tell them to choose a topic and write about it without allowing children to talk first about the topic. Some teachers may choose a prompt and ask children to add ideas, again without discussing it first. These teachers are then surprised when their students respond with stares or confused looks, or with one-sentence writing like, "I like my cat."

Here's how one first-year, first-grade teacher explained her experiences asking young children to choose a topic for writing. "I tell them to write about whatever they want," she said. "If they choose computers, I tell them to write about what they like about computers. But they just sit there!"

Another teacher, a veteran second-grade teacher, described writer's workshop in her classroom this way: "It's like pulling teeth trying to get these kids to write," she said. "I sit there and ask repeatedly, 'And then what happened? And then what happened?' "

As these experiences with student writing demonstrate, young children do not simply think and then write—they are still learning how to use words to formulate and articulate their thoughts. They are working to make letter-sound connections, to remember what each letter looks like, to spell correctly, to reproduce the letter physically, and to use correct punctuation.

To prevent frustrating writing experiences, do not send your students to their seats to stare at a blank piece of paper. Help them, through engaged conversation, to begin the task of writing with their words already spoken and, therefore, ready in their minds to be transposed into writing on the page before them.

When you give children the opportunity to articulate their ideas conversationally with an interested listener before beginning to write, they approach writing with eagerness. Moreover, as children develop thoughts through conversation, ideas for writing are within easy reach. The conversation gives them a mental map, which guides and motivates them as they practice the mechanical aspects of writing and learn specific craft skills.

The following list describes the process through which children move from thinking to speaking to writing. It suggests how thoughtful, open-ended questions encourage that process.

Thoughts ("I'm thinking about my cat.")
Verbal expression of thoughts ("I have a cat.")
Teacher asking open-ended questions about ideas ("I don't have a cat! Will you tell me about what the best part of having a cat is?")
Response to teacher's question ("Feeding her.")
Elaboration on the child's words ("You feed your cat? What do you feed her? Do you also give her water to drink? It sounds like you take good care of her!")
Rehearsing her words to prepare for writing ("Let's figure out the words you are going to write about your cat. You told me that you feed your cat tuna and water. How about, 'I feed my cat wet tuna food and I give it water.'"?)
Writing the words down

Conversations with Reluctant Talkers

Almost every class includes children who eagerly offer their thoughts to the large group and those who wait to offer their ideas until most of the class has gone to their seats to begin writing. After my first invitation to "whoever is ready to write" to leave the meeting area to begin writing, I usually find that the remaining students are more willing to talk when fewer children are in

I Do Not Like

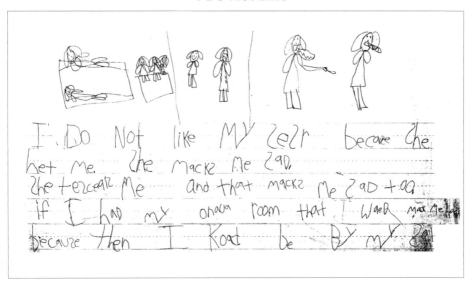

When children write from experiences of their lives, the topics are authentic and meaningful.

the group. In fact, many teachers have told me that these moments were the first time they heard these particular children speak.

Other children choose not to speak but will reassure me that they know about what they are going to write. They are able to generate ideas as they listen. Whether they are shy, native speakers, or non-native speakers who simply are not confident enough with their English, this group of children often responds to the opportunity to express their ideas and thoughts through drawing and writing.

One morning in a first-grade classroom, I approached a little girl who sat silently at her seat, and I asked her if she was feeling all right. She answered that she was tired because she stayed up late with her sister. Pleased that she was sharing something with me, I pursued the conversation, hoping to help her find a topic for writing.

"What's it like having a sister?" I asked.

Without pausing, she blurted out, "Terrible!"

There was her topic! She wrote, "I do not like my sister because she hits me.

She makes me sad. She teases me and that makes me sad too. If I had my own room it would make me happy because then I could be by myself."

Conversations with "Safe" Writers

Some children will write the same sentence day after day. They are afraid to stray from writing words they know how to spell. In the process, they lose their sense of engagement with their writing and their enthusiasm.

As you help your students verbally explore their thoughts, feelings, and experiences, be attentive not only to what topics delight and please them but also to what troubles them. The opportunity to express difficult emotions conversationally can motivate children to write and help them to cope with hardship, loss, grief, disappointment, anxiety, fear, outrage, and any number of similarly difficult emotions. Sonia Nieto, in her 2002 book, *Language, Culture, and Teaching*, finds, "Teachers who allow children to articulate troubling issues find that their life experiences serve as valuable assets to their writing, rather than handicaps to learning."

Here's an example. A first-grade ELL student named Talia would write her signature, safe sentence, "I went to the park," day after day. One day, however, she stopped writing, looked up at me, and said anxiously," I saw a picture of a bad boy. He takes kids."

I remembered a letter and a police sketch the school system sent to all families in the county, alerting them to a suspicious person in the area. I then asked her to tell me more about the picture. She proceeded to talk rapidly about the sketch and about her fears.

I explained to her that something important and powerful that we are thinking and feeling is usually a good topic to choose for our writing. Good writers, I told her, often choose topics about which they care or have strong feelings. I said that it didn't make sense to write about one thing while she was thinking about something else. After our conversation, Talia turned the page of her writing notebook, abandoned her park theme, and, instead, wrote enthusiastically on a new page about how she felt when she saw the flyer with the picture of the "bad boy."

When we encourage students to feel at ease sharing their thoughts, feelings, and experiences, they begin to find their way as writers, expressing themselves first in conversation and, soon after, in writing.

Conversations with English Language Learners

A class meeting that emphasizes conversation, as described in Chapter 4, offers an opportunity to monitor whether your ELL children are silent or listening and how well they are expressing themselves in their new language. Be sure to respond enthusiastically to any efforts at speaking.

Be careful not to shame these students because of difficulties they may have with spoken English. As you teach these children to write, also remember that they will become fluent in their new language in the same way your own children learned their first language: by hearing and by using it. As a teacher of children who are learning English, you should keep the following in mind:

- As ELL children learn English, they are simultaneously learning a new culture. The process takes time!
- We have to allow ELL children to speak more so that they have the opportunity to try out the words they are hearing.
- No matter what we are teaching and no matter how trivial it seems, we have to speak and listen to ELL children with respect and attention.

Experts of child development, as well as those of us who have children, are familiar with the "Why?" stage that two- and three-year-olds go through. Almost everything a child says at this stage begins with a demanding, "Why?" Such questions need responses that provide them with opportunities to learn new information and new vocabulary. For our second language learners, we need to recreate the "Why?" stage in the classroom.

Talk aloud. To help your ELL students build vocabulary in their new language, provide a running commentary in your classroom. Name objects. Describe processes. Give reasons and detailed explanations. Your ELL students may hear a lot of English spoken on the television at home, but TV and radio will not provide them (or their parents) with enough understandable language to allow them to learn much English.

Speak simply. Remember that children learning a second language need to hear simple sentences spoken slowly and repeatedly. Try to avoid colloquialisms, slang, and difficult figures of speech. Such expressions, which are common on TV, may confuse ELL children. As much as possible, show the meaning of your words and phrases with physical props, illustrations, gestures, and facial expressions.

Encourage ELL students to talk. When they are ready to speak in English, encourage them to participate in conversation during the class meeting. These children need opportunities to practice the English-language words they hear spoken around them. By participating conversationally in the class meeting, they can practice using English words to express the ideas, feelings, and experiences that are important to them and will, therefore, be their best topics for writing.

Get to know them. Also build up your background knowledge of these students and their culture. Make a point, especially, to learn about their immigration experiences, which are likely to be a vivid memory for them. Find out with whom they are living now that they are in the U.S.

Get to know their cultures. Try to be sensitive to the differences between the children's home cultures and American culture. For example, I once saw a father correct his daughter when she gave me a gift using her left hand. Later I learned that extending the left hand to another person is considered disrespectful in their culture. Similarly, I had a Korean student who would never look me in the eye. While avoiding eye contact with a

The Earthquake

There was an earthquake in El Salvador. Hundreds of people died. All the people cried. Some people died and people were sad because they missed their families and their babies, too. I want to go to El Salvador to see what's wrong. I will help all the peop in El Salvador and help them a lot. And I will help my family. I will bring them food and drink. I will bring them good things.

After participating in conversations, children will use these discussions as topics in their writing.

teacher is considered evasive and rude in this country, it is common practice for children in Korea to show respect for adults, including teachers, by not looking at them directly.

As you get to know your ELL students, your discussions with them can reflect their life experiences. While you will want all students to make a meaningful connection between writing and their experiences and ideas, such connections are especially important for children learning a new language. Research shows that children more quickly acquire a new language—including learning to write in the new language—when they make meaningful connections between their own experiences and the new language. The authors of *Because Writing Matters*, the 2003 report by the National Writing Project, assert:

> Student writing develops within a context of discourse—that is, a system of values, beliefs, norms, and behaviors that is inherently social . . . learning a new language, in addition to being a grammatical task, also asks the student to take on a new identity. Writing instruction succeeds when the new identity of the students does not oppose home culture.
>
> Writing research has shown us that learning to write involves not only learning the process of inquiry, drafting, revising, and editing, but also a web of relationships between a child and her peers, home life and the wider culture, or a child's culture and that of the school. The research suggests that the best writing teaching simultaneously supports the child's home identity while promoting success in school. (p. 29)

All children, especially children who are not native-English speakers, need opportunities to talk about their ideas, to respond to interested questions about what they have said, and to think about which words they would like to say and eventually to write.

Making Time for Conversation

Since conversation is powerful, make the most of every opportunity. This can begin the minute young writers walk through the door; at that moment, you begin to teach them writing.

You can use virtually any activity to generate conversation. A Maryland elementary school where I worked began serving a free breakfast to all children in classes during the first 20 minutes of the day. Since I knew that some children often came to school hungry, I welcomed the breakfast program. I was relieved to know that the empty stomachs of my students would no longer distract them during our morning class time. But some teachers resented the mess the cereal created or resented the time that breakfast took away from "instruction."

Others, however, used this time to problem-solve with their students, showing them, for instance, how to open the cereal box with scissors to avoid spilling. The breakfast program became an opportunity for family-style meals, a time to enjoy informal conversations with the children. In one K-1 classroom that serves the needs of children with language-development delays, the teacher and the school's speech therapist spent breakfast sitting and chatting with the students.

This daily routine gave these students opportunities to listen, to speak, and to begin each day in a relaxed, comfortable atmosphere. When the children sat down to write later in the day, they often chose topics they had talked about during conversation over breakfast.

Listening to our students may seem uncomfortably counterintuitive, especially with the curriculum we each feel pressed to cover and all those new writing concepts we want to introduce. However, if we do not show that we are interested in what our students have to say, how can we expect them to believe we are interested in what they write?

When you take time to talk with your students, to inquire about their lives and to listen to what they tell you, your time is well spent. The youngest student learns to write by talking first. Such exchanges provide students with the valuable experience of using words to communicate the thoughts, feelings, and experiences that matter most to them to an attentive, interested listener.

As your students talk, listen. Learn about their lives outside of school, their personal experiences, their thoughts and feelings, their hobbies and other special interests, and their concerns. Focus on each of them, on not only the children most likely to grab your attention, children with behavioral problems and children who are academic stars. When you get to know each of your students as the son or daughter and brother or sister they are every day and explore their interests and dreams, you begin to help each one find the best and most meaningful topics for writing.

To find out how well you know each of your students, take a moment for the

If I Could Fly

IF I Could Fly...

IF I could Fly I would go to El Salvador and I would visit my grandma and grandpa. I do not know them but I saw pictures of them. The pictures made me feel happy becuse I could see what they look like. I have four grandperents Who I never met. I think they would hug me and kiss me if they saw me Then I would take them to where I live. I would Show them my sisten and my mom and my dad and I would tell them about my uncles that live close by. Then I would show them my school. I would talk with them in spanish. I love them even if I dont know them.

following exercise, recommended by educator and author Donald Graves in his book, *Writing: Teachers and Children at Work.* List the name of each student in your class without looking at your class roster. Next, name one or two special interests or concerns each child considers important. Now ask yourself whether you have discussed any of the topics with the child to let him or her know that you are aware of and interested in these special interests and concerns. If you have not, make a point to do so.

Now consider the following interaction that I observed between a kindergartner and her teacher when I was a graduate student. Because I documented this conversation to use in a paper I was writing at the time, the dialogue represents the exact words of the child and the teacher.

Elizabeth was sitting in a show-and-tell semicircle with her classmates when the teacher asked who would like to share. Several children raised their hands, and the teacher called on Elizabeth. The teacher pulled her onto her lap, and Elizabeth began to talk about her experiences over the recent Thanksgiving holiday. When she paused in her account, however, the teacher interrupted her.

"You forgot to bring something in for show-and-tell, so you want to just talk?" the teacher asked. Elizabeth nodded.

But her teacher replied, "No! This is the third time, Elizabeth! What do you think will happen next year in first grade if you forget things? Go back to your seat. Nobody else forgets. Why do you?"

This teacher's punitive reaction was undoubtedly humiliating. And while "show-and-tell" usually does involve showing an object and then discussing it, a young child's sense of being valued is far more important than following a rigid format. While the rules of show-and-tell may be broken, a child's self-esteem should not be. Elizabeth—and all the other students—learned that mere stories from Elizabeth's life were not valued or of any interest.

As a teacher, you exert tremendous influence over every child in your classroom. Every interaction between you and your student is an opportunity for that student either to learn and feel validated or to be shamed and feel humiliated. The strong influence teachers exert in their students' lives is a topic child psychologist Dr. Haim Ginott writes about in his book *Between Teacher and Child.*

> I have come to a frightening conclusion. I am the decisive element in the classroom. It is my personal approach that creates the climate. . . . As a teacher, I possess tremendous power to make a child's life miserable or joyous. I can be a tool of torture or an instrument of inspiration. I can humiliate or humor, hurt, or heal.

If a child does not believe that the topics that interest and concern him most are important or interesting to his teacher, he will not draw upon them for writing topics. Instead, he will say, "I don't know what to write about." His teacher will be compelled to offer an idea for writing, which may not motivate that child to write.

When we are interested and caring listeners, students become motivated to learn skills. If we lack empathy for or show little interest in their experiences, ideas, hopes, and dreams, their eagerness to express themselves through writing is likely to wane. By honoring the content of the personal writing of young children—the ideas, thoughts, and feelings of their lives— we can, as teachers, build a solid foundation of trust upon which skills find a fertile place to grow.

Using the Classroom to Engage Young Writers

Begin to examine the structure and layout of your classroom. Think of using the physical environment of your classroom as an important scaffolding technique that supports student development. Planning the arrangement of your classroom to support writing instruction can have a dramatic influence on your students. A carefully arranged classroom can help writers to begin to use strategies that older, capable writers apply naturally. Here are several key features.

Alphabet strips with pictures taped on to each desk/table. As children develop phonetic spelling skills, listening for the sounds in words and writing down the corresponding letters, alphabet strips support their efforts to write letters and spell words.

A "word wall" displaying high-frequency words. Reading researchers have discovered that 100 high-frequency words make up half of all the words we read and write. When children can write these words easily and without much thought, they gain confidence and try to spell words that are more difficult. Knowing the correct spelling for the high-frequency words means children can devote more of their attention to the many other skills a good writer needs to have in addition to spelling. As students become fluent with high-frequency words, the writing process takes less effort and becomes more enjoyable.

These 100 words were first identified in *Spelling K-8* (Snowball and Bolton). Some of these words children need to master by the end of kindergarten and the rest by the end of first grade. A vivid classroom display of these words will help young students memorize the correct spelling for each one.

Since the word wall functions as a quick reference source for your students as they write, make sure the children can see it—placed at eye level and with words listed far enough apart to be read easily.

To encourage your students to refer to the word wall, be sure to use this learning aid daily in games, lessons, and instruction. Rhyming is one example of a word-wall game you can play with your students. You might say, "I'm thinking of a word that rhymes with 'book' and starts with an 'L.' Who can find the rhyming word on the word wall?" One good source for ideas for games to use with the word wall is *Phonics They Use* by Patricia Cunningham.

High-Frequency Words for Kindergartners to Learn

a	am	an	and	at
come	Go	here	I	in
is	It	Like	look	me
my	see	the	this	to
up	We			

Additional High-Frequency Words for First Graders and Second Graders

about	After	all	are	As
back	Be	because	been	Big
but	By	came	can	could
day	did	do	down	First
for	From	get	going	Got
had	has	have	he	her
here	him	his	if	Into
just	Little	made	make	More
no	Not	now	of	Off
on	one	only	or	Our
out	over	said	saw	she
so	some	that	their	Them
then	There	they	this	those
very	was	went	were	What
when	Which	who	why	Will
would	you	your		

Young students model teacher behavior, and they quickly learn what parts of the curriculum the teacher considers most important. Therefore, as a part of your writing instruction, be sure to emphasize the value of learning the high-frequency words. If you use the word wall in your classroom, your students will, too.

Children's Self-Published Books

Publishing books can motivate and excite the children. When you "publish" your students' writing and proudly place the resulting "books" in your classroom library, your young writers turn to their own past writing for spelling support and as a source of ideas for future writing.

These books are particularly helpful for struggling readers, who may have difficulty reading other books in the classroom. When such children see the words they have written in their own book, they are likely to remember what they wrote and can, as a result, accurately read the words in their published books, even if they can't yet read them elsewhere. In this way, the words in your young students' published books become an important reinforcement for their reading, as well as their writing vocabularies.

Additionally, your students will benefit from reading each other's published books. In my classroom, I keep my students' self-published books on a shelf labeled, "Local Authors." These books are available for student reading along with the rest of the books for children in my classroom. A shelf that features student books helps children regard themselves and each other as authors.

I was recently delighted to hear one of my students, a six-year-old named Sharon, describe herself and her classmates as "authors." Sharon confidently told me, "All authors, including children like us, get ideas from their lives."

Poems and Songs and Big Books. Word walls display alphabetical lists of high-frequency words. Big books and poems and songs that children know provide a place to find the words in context. Write them on large chart paper and display them when the children sing. You can then use the words of the song to point out high-frequency words that the children are expected to learn, and they learn them within the context of the entire text.

A Quiet Work Place. A quiet classroom helps children maintain their focus and engage in their writing. Essentially, it helps them do their best.

Be vigilant about reducing the noise level in the classroom during writing workshop. Remember, if you want your students to work quietly, you, too, must be quiet.

While students are writing, don't distract them with reminders such as "Don't forget to use the word wall" or "Remember to cross out mistakes and keep writing." Children receive a conflicting message about the need for silence while writing if *you* speak loudly while they are writing. They need a quiet place to think and to show you what they can do.

It is, of course, necessary and important to talk with your young writers about their work in progress and to hold individual conferences with them at their seats. You will need to read your students' writing, show them you are interested in what they have written, and ask meaningful questions to help them revise and improve their writing. But such conversations need to occur quietly, with soft voices, so the hard work of writing, which is ongoing throughout the classroom, will not be interrupted.

Organize Writing Papers. Young writers need an organized place to store their writing pieces. Two-pocket folders inevitably create a disorganized mess for kindergartners . Instead, I recommend that you staple together several pages of "storybook paper," which has lines for writing and a space for drawing. Attach a construction-paper cover. All simple revising can be done within this homemade workbook. If a particular piece is chosen to be used through all steps of the writing process (which will be discussed in more detail later), you can give that child a separate, single sheet of paper on which to do so.

To help first and second graders keep their writing papers in order, use a pocket folder. Label the left side of the folder "Rough Drafts," and label the right side "Revisions and Edits." If they decide to develop a piece of writing for publication, they can move the paper out of the left pocket and into the right pocket. Any rough drafts that they do not want to revise can be thrown out, taken home, or saved for a later date.

Once your students have suitable folders for storing their writing papers, you can then spend a few minutes with each child to review the folder's contents to help the child choose which pieces of writing to keep, which to develop through further revision, and which to abandon and throw out. A good time for this kind of review is before writer's workshop. It also can be the subject of a mini-lesson presented before children begin to write.

Use the Writing Process to Support Writing. It is important to introduce the writing process in the early-writing classroom. The writing process teaches children the structure of writing: pre-writing, drafting, revising, editing, and publishing. They learn how to work on a piece over a period of time and how to work independently. They learn how to make responsible choices regarding their work rather than waiting for directions. If, for example, a child's hand is tired from writing, she knows that she can take a break and work on editing a piece to check her spelling using the words on the word wall. The writing process framework functions, in effect, as a classroom management technique.

Jennifer Williams, a second grade teacher, requires that her students take responsibility for certain elements of the writing process. She tells her students, for example, that they need to reread their rough draft before showing it to her. She demonstrates how a writer rereads a piece of writing and "thinks aloud" about how to make improvements. The children then proceed to reread their own writing and make improvements. Jennifer tells of a little girl who reread her work, found that she had left out a word, and proudly announced, "Look! First I forgot to put 'it'! But now it makes sense!"

As children become more capable writers, they can spend more time on each step of the writing process. Even the earliest writers, however, should be taught the steps of the writing process and strategies for approaching each step. Learning the steps becomes an end in itself, a skill that children can begin to acquire in kindergarten. With each lesson, teachers can explain to children which step in the writing process they are working on, so that children will learn each step and eventually be able to take a piece of writing from rough draft to publishing almost independently.

Teach Writing Craft. During the writer's workshop, teaching elements of the writing craft helps a child understand specific techniques that all writers use to make their writing better. Teachers must model different craft elements—from the many ways that start or end a piece, or to vary sentence structure, or to add specific details—so that the child understands the techniques and practices them during writer's workshop. As writing educator Marcia Freeman noted in 1986, "Writing process is what writers do. Writing craft is what they know."

With the writer-friendly environment in place, the next step is to assess the skill level of each child. In the next chapter, you will find three assessment strategies that gauge students' writing abilities and monitor their progress throughout the school year.

Assessing Writing Behavior and Writing Progress

I n the current discussion of the value of standardized testing, the central issue has been lost. Instead of asking, "*Should* we test young children?" more valuable questions might be, "What are our expectations of our student's learning?" and "*How* can we appropriately, validly, and reliably assess them to ensure that they are, in fact, learning?"

The two types of writing assessments that follow provide useful information about the writing abilities of young students. The first, an informal anecdotal assessment, gives a picture of what I call the *writing behavior* of a student. A second, more formal writing assessment based on prompts given three times a year, gives teachers, administrators, and parents information about a child's *growth* in writing and whether the child is meeting grade-level expectations.

Understanding Children's Writing Behavior

By the time some children enter kindergarten, they have already learned a lot about writing behavior from watching their parents and older siblings. If they have opportunities to imitate positive models of writing behavior at home, they have an advantage when they begin learning to write in school.

They have learned, for example, that people cannot talk and write at the same time. They know that when people are writing, they often request silence because writing takes thought, time, and effort. Finally, they understand that people write to share their ideas with others.

Other children arrive in kindergarten with few early experiences of modeled writing behavior. They begin school without the most basic knowledge of what writing is or how and even why it is undertaken. A preliminary assessment of writing behavior makes sense especially when teaching writing to these learners.

Children display many different reactions when they sit down to write. They differ in their ability to focus their thoughts, choose a topic, use spelling resources available in the classroom, write independently, and maintain the attention needed to complete a piece of writing.

Good writing behavior generally indicates a good writer. After observing young writers at work in my classrooms, I created this list of counter-productive behaviors that get in the way of good writing. I then developed some intervention strategies. I encourage you to use this list to target and correct the specific writing-behavior problems that impede the progress of your young writers. Use Chart 1.1, on page 19, to record your observations, to identify children who need help learning successful learning behaviors, and to note specific interventions to try with each child.

Note: Halfway through kindergarten, most children are expected to write quietly and independently, read what they have written, add more ideas to their writing, and check the word wall for the correct spelling of high frequency words. My list of writing behaviors, therefore, is geared toward first and second graders and kindergartners who are ready for independent writing.

Stopping Writing to Erase. As children write their rough drafts, they need to understand that their goal is to get their ideas onto paper. If they spend time erasing, they may lose their focus and stop the flow of thoughts.

To prevent such distraction, model how to cross out errors with one quick line and then continue writing.

Taking away the erasers is another way to keep children writing. I have seen teachers remove eraser tips from pencils or give students thick pencils made without erasers for writing rough drafts. Later, when children work on their final drafts—after editing their work—they can use erasers to produce neat final drafts.

Talking and Fidgeting. As discussed in the last chapter, talking definitely prepares young children to write. Nevertheless, students' conversations should occur at specific times. When children stop writing to discuss

Name	Date	Observations	Follow-Up

their writing topics, it may mean they have not orally explored their ideas sufficiently before they began to write.

A good way to make sure students are ready to begin writing is to ask what the first sentence of the composition will be. When children can answer this question easily, they are ready to begin to write. If they cannot answer this question, additional conversation about their ideas may help them to imagine and anticipate what they will write.

Emergent writers need a lot of support. You can ask them what words they are going to write, count the words with them, and discuss how they will figure out how to write each word. If their sentence is, for example, "I play soccer at the park," you might respond with, "Let's count your words." Use your fingers to indicate that six words are contained in that sentence. Then ask the child what the first word to write in the sentence is, and use the word wall to help establish that the first word is "I." For the second word, "play," remind the child how to do sound-spelling.

You can also point out the alphabet strip on their table as a resource. When children are clear about the direct connection between talking and writing, when they have prepared their words orally before they begin putting these words on paper, they are more likely to sit quietly and write. To help them remain focused on their writing, teach them to reread their sentence or sentences once they have finished their rough drafts. Let them know that they can also look over their drawings and think about what else to add to the pictures or their pieces before they ask for help.

Asking the Teacher How to Spell Words. Spelling is an integral part of writing and important for children to learn. If children are anxious about spelling every word correctly, however, they will be inhibited about writing even a rough draft for fear of making a spelling mistake.

To help young writers overcome anxiety about spelling every word correctly the first time they write it, explain and model the process of using "sound spelling" and thinking about spelling patterns they already know. Let them know that the spelling can be checked and corrected later, when they edit and revise their rough drafts. During the first months, be sure to edit their rough drafts as soon as possible. This way you will relieve their anxiety about having any misspelled words on their pages.

You may also want to examine how you teach high-frequency words and use the word wall. If your students are misspelling the high-frequency words you have already taught, address these spelling problems immediately. First-grade children should be held responsible for correct spelling of the known high-frequency words even on their rough drafts. Mastering these words is likely to reassure them, and they can reserve their mental energy for addressing unknown words.

Assessment with School-Wide K-2 Prompts

Daily writing offers opportunities for you to make frequent observations about and informal assessment of their students' writing abilities. A more formal, school-wide writing assessment is also necessary to understand their writing levels. After all, during writing time every day, we offer students help and suggestions as they write, so we may not always have a good idea of what they can do independently.

School-level assessment that is designed, administered, and analyzed by the teachers and administrators of the school gives you a fair and useful way to determine progress in writing, especially for the primary grades. The teachers and administrators in a school must have a picture of the independent abilities of students, which they will use to evaluate the learning needs of students and to plan their instructional programs. Especially for lower grades, assessments are needed to compare children *at the same school* because baselines between one school and another can vary greatly.

Since children enter kindergarten with widely varying preschool experiences and literary exposure from home, early educators need to determine the starting point of each child and to move each child toward academic standards in a systematic way—*based on the actual progress of that child.* Some children need extra time to meet those standards because their starting point was so far behind that of other children.

Make no mistake. All children can meet the standards and should be expected to do so. But the task of "catch-up" does take time, and school-based assessments during the early childhood years of school help educators to assess more accurately real progress that may not be reflected in standardized testing that happens district-wide.

Jim Cummins (1979) found that children learning a second language need about five years to master academic English. By third grade, children who have been in school since Head Start are in their fifth year of school and can be fairly compared to their native English-speaking peers. Internal assessments created by schools and districts take language acquisition variability into account and introduce performance standards while recognizing individual growth.

With the formal assessment, the guidelines are consistent in each classroom. They include the direction that teachers should not provide any help once children have begun to write. A consistently applied school-wide writing assessment gathers data by child, class, and grade-level and helps a school determine the overall quality of its instructional program for writing.

Moreover, since the primary purpose of gathering data is to guide instruction, a school-wide assessment identifies areas of strength and need and helps us determine the school's instructional direction. Because all the stages of the assessment process occur within the school, results are available within a few weeks, and teachers are able to plan their instruction based on those results.

Most important, because the assessments are based on sequential, developmental stages, children who are not yet meeting the grade-level standard can still show growth and improvement, giving teachers and parents real reason to celebrate. This is critically important for early childhood teachers in Title I schools who are teaching the youngest and poorest children. Without encouragement, frustration easily builds, and morale can suffer.

Components of School-Based Writing Assessment

The writing assessment includes the following elements:

- Three writing prompts administered school-wide to all K-2 students: given at the beginning of the year, in January, and in May or June.
- A scoring rubric designed to assess emergent writers.
- Two scoring rubrics to assess early writers: one for writing goals, the other for conventions.
- Classroom teachers scoring their own students.
- A second scorer for all papers.
- Collaborative planning between classroom teachers and the second scorer to achieve agreement of scores and consistency in school-wide scoring.

The Writing Prompts

This assessment tool measures students three times: in September for baseline data, in January to track progress, and at the end of the school year to provide a writing sample for the child's new teacher. The final samples also help the school evaluate improvement in its overall writing performance.

For best results, I strongly recommend that all teachers give the same prompt. Presenting the same prompt to all students minimizes the inevitable subjectivity in scoring the writing. Comparisons among papers are easier to make because the topic remains consistent. Teachers are able to identify more easily students who struggle to find a topic, to develop their ideas, or to maintain organization in their writing.

Because children at this age have such varying reading levels, the prompt is administered orally. Teachers read the prompt aloud as many times as necessary and with as much explanation as needed to enable students to begin to write on the topic. Students focus on writing, not reading the prompt or trying to understand it.

Eliminating reading as a factor is extremely important. Primary children possess dramatically varied reading abilities. Some children find a written copy of the prompt helpful; for others who struggle with reading, the written prompt can cause distraction and anxiety.

Having said that, however, writing in response to text *is* an important skill and one that we *should* teach and assess. We should regard it, however, as a separate genre of writing, one that includes analyzing new information contained in the text, and, therefore, assesses more than writing ability. When assessing writing in response to text, teachers should present text that is matched to each child's reading level, or is slightly below it, thus isolating the written response skill.

Topics for the Prompt

The topics of the prompt should be based on school experiences so that children's varied life experiences do not enter into the assessment and to eliminate cultural or socio-economic bias. Even the seemingly benign question, "What did you do over the summer?" emphasizes the enormous gap between a child who went to the beach with his family and a child who sat in a hot apartment watching television.

On the other hand, when we ask about a favorite day at school or about what the children have learned, the topic emerges from a repertoire of shared experiences. By basing the prompt on an experience children shared at school in the recent past, we are also tapping into the concrete nature of young children's thinking. Most children aged five to seven are still unable to think in abstract ways, and would, therefore, struggle with a prompt that asks them to write about a theoretical situation.

For example, the question, "What would you see at the zoo?" will probably lead young children to talk about an actual trip to the zoo instead of pondering all the hypothetical possibilities based on what he knows about zoos. Of course, the question leaves behind those children who have never been to a zoo or cannot remember very much about a time they did visit a zoo.

Sample Prompts

Here are several examples of prompts used with K-2 children that deal with concrete experiences that they have all shared.

- Think about some of your favorite things that you do at school. Choose one of your favorite things and draw and write all about it.
- There are many teachers and other adults at school who help you and care about you. Choose and write about one of them. As you write, tell who the person is, and explain the ways he or she helps you and cares about you.
- We have all learned many interesting and exciting things in school this year. Think about something that you have learned and tell all about what you learned.
- We have had many special days at school. We had Math Day, Valentine's Day, Young Author's Conference, some fun field trips, and many other special days. Choose a day that you liked the best and write all about it.

Directions for Administering the Prompt

Here are some points to remember when administering the school-wide prompt.

- The writing prompt is intended to give the school a picture of the students' writing abilities, including their abilities to express their thoughts on paper and to demonstrate understanding of writing. This exercise is not intended to simulate any standardized test, nor is it intended to reflect reading or listening comprehension.

- The prompt should be completed all in one sitting to minimize any interruption in the children's focus and concentration.
- Make sure the children have all necessary materials before they begin. Have some extra sharpened pencils so that they do not have to get up to sharpen them. If children usually draw before they begin to write, allow them to do so.
- Read the prompt aloud—more than once, if necessary. Teachers should not answer questions about the mechanics or content of the children's writing once they have started, but they can clarify anything that prevents a child from engaging in the exercise. For example, if a child does not begin to write, you may say, "Tell me about some things you do in school. Now choose one of them to write about." Do not make a suggestion for them, such as, "Why don't you write about recess?"
- This is an untimed assessment. If, however, a child spends more than ten minutes drawing a picture, then say, "I would like you to start writing now."
- A teacher will score her own students' papers, and then give the class papers to a colleague, who will be the second scorer. (School administrators can select a staff member to be the second scorer.)

Assessment Criteria

Criteria to judge the writing of young children must be identified before writing can be assessed. Our expectations should involve seeing our young writers incorporate age-appropriate writing skills. What, then, are the major characteristics that comprise writing?

Characteristics of good writing:

- addressing specific audiences with an expressive voice
- selecting descriptive, engaging words
- varying sentence types and lengths
- selecting ideas and developing those ideas
- organizing the ideas
- using correct conventions such as spelling, punctuation, and grammar

The characteristics of writing comprise the common thread that runs through all the writing we do, and there are several ways to arrange them. The AEIOU system that I developed helps us remember the basic categories.

It is also the basis for the various rubrics that follow later in this and the next chapters and for the writing-goal lessons in Chapter 5.

A - Addressing your Audience: The young writer's awareness that others will be reading her work and the extent to which she expresses her unique "voice" to her readers with the explanation of her feelings and actions, and use of first, second, and third person pronouns. (Young children demonstrate the use of "voice" through their natural excitement and enthusiasm. By alerting them to specific craft techniques in their writing and in the writing of their peers, we can begin to teach them to use voice consciously.)

E - Expression of language: The young writer's ability to create writing that is fluid and pleasant to read, through word choice and sentence variety and phrasing

I - Ideas: The writer's clear statements of ideas and supporting details to explain those ideas

O - Organization: The way the ideas are connected, sequenced, and ordered, including the use of an opening sentence or "hook," and the use of a concluding or summarizing sentence

U - Understanding Conventions: the writer's correct use of spelling, punctuation, capitalization, and grammar

Honoring the Emergent Writer's Journey

Our youngest writers are just learning that writing is a way to communicate. The earliest writers may scribble, may represent a word with only a single letter, or they may leave out letters in a word they try to write. They are mastering many different, complex skills, and while they are in this stage of experimenting for their own pleasure and practice, concentrating on the need of the reader to understand their messages is not their top priority.

Because they are just beginning to learn how to write and may still be scribbling, drawing exclusively, or writing approximations of letters, assessment criteria for them should be limited. Young writers are just beginning to write and may still be scribbling, writing approximations of letters, or even exclusively drawing. Therefore, assessment criteria for them should be limited. Trying to apply standards of literary style or organization of text to emergent writing, for example, is at best meaningless and at worst detrimental for the learner.

We would not try to evaluate the swimming stroke of a child doing doggy-paddle. We might praise, however, a new swimmer's confidence and ability to move across the pool independently and encourage her to blow bubbles as she swims. Similarly, trying to analyze the organization or writing style demonstrated by a child who writes two words to accompany a picture is artificial. There simply is not enough writing on the page to analyze.

Analyzing the *spacing* of those two words on the paper, however, tells a great deal about the young writer's budding knowledge of basic writing conventions. Furthermore, looking at the relationship between the picture and the writing provides valuable information about how well the child understands that writing is used to communicate ideas.

Drawing a parallel between emergent writers and emergent readers, my friend and colleague, Floyd Starnes, points out that an early emergent book, with one line of large print per page and a repetitive sentence pattern, does not offer enough information for an in-depth discussion about the young reader's comprehension of the text, or of her life experiences.

While we must make sure, of course, that the child *understands the message* contained in the words, we will spend our instructional time on strategies appropriate for emergent readers. For example, has the child acquired one-to-one correspondence? Does she use the pictures to help identify unknown words? Does he use meaning and structure to predict an unknown word and then crosscheck by looking at the first letter?

By deliberately and consciously looking at emergent writers *separately* from young writers who are beginning to use more complex writing skills, we recognize and acknowledge the enormous strides in learning that these beginning writers demonstrate. If we judge them with the same standards as we use for more advanced writers, emergent writers appear to be *lacking* in ability, and our perception is that they are "behind" the rest. If we look at them at their own stage of writing development, we celebrate each small step they take, understanding that they are well on their way to mastering the complex body of knowledge that is the English language.

Looked at in this way, emergent writers are able to depict some notion of, and be assessed on, "*understanding conventions*" and "*ideas*."

As explained by Marie Clay (1975), children progress through sequential stages of writing, which I have grouped based on the two writing characteristics as follows:

Content of Ideas: "I have something to tell."
The emergent writer communicates an idea with

- Scribbles
- Pictures
- Approximations of letters with no decipherable message (The child may or may not share the message verbally, but the writing cannot stand alone.)
- Letters that represent the first sound of each word
- Word label or phrase (My cat; me; mommy; red flower)
- Complete sentence (I love my dad)

English Conventions: The "grapho-phonic" features of English, including letter formation, spacing on the page, spelling, capitalization, and punctuation. The emergent writer shows developing understanding of the conventions of English with the following activities:

- **Scribbles:** A child who is scribbling is experimenting with the writing tool and is still developing fine-motor control.
- **Emergent Letters:** A child who is forming emergent letters is becoming aware of the features of English letters and is attempting to reproduce the print that she sees around her.
- **Conventional letters:** A child who forms letters correctly has internalized the English alphabet (usually capital letters).
- **Left to right direction across the page:** A child who writes from left to write understands that this is the standard English way to place writing on a piece of paper.
- **More than one row of left to right writing:** A child who writes to the end of a line and then begins on the left side of the page for the second line of writing has learned the skill described by Marie Clay as "return sweep."
- **Creative spelling:** A child who uses creative spelling demonstrates awareness of the sounds in words (phonemes) and the letters that represent each sound (phonics).
- **Conventional spelling:** A child who uses some conventional spelling has internalized the visual characteristics of individual words and understands that words are always spelled the same way.

- **Spaces between words:** A child who can space the words appropriately on the page without running them together shows further understanding of the way English is written.
- **Use of capitals at the beginning of a sentence:** A child who uses capitals to begin sentences shows an understanding of the elements of a complete sentence and of how written English is supposed to appear on paper.
- **Use of ending punctuation:** A child who uses ending punctuation shows further understanding of the elements of a complete sentence and has some idea of the different types of sentences.

The rubric below provides assessment data on individual children, class, grade level, and school progress. Samples of children at each rubric level follow.

Emergent Stages of Writing Scoring Rubric

SCORE	CHARACTERISTICS
5	One or more complete sentences Ending punctuation Beginning capitalization Spaces between words Conventional and creative spelling
4	Complete sentence Conventional and creative spelling
3	Word or phrase Conventional and creative spelling Left to right row of conventional letters
2	No decipherable message Picture Random emergent and conventional letters
1	No decipherable message Scribbles Random emergent letters

Writing Samples of Emergent Writers

Emergent Level 1

Emergent Level 2

Emergent Level 3

Emergent Level 4

Emergent Level 5

Importance of Emergent Rubrics

A separate rubric that recognizes and honors the characteristics and capabilities of emergent writers allows us to see growth that might not be perceived by the more advanced rubrics designed for "early" writers. At the beginning of first grade, for example, a few first graders may well be at the skill level of an emergent writer. Yet, before our school used the specific rubric for emergent writers, we were using rubrics assigned to grade levels, and so scored all first graders with the "first- and second-grade rubric." The result? Emergent writers scored a "0."

The following year, we adapted specific emergent-writer rubrics which matched the rubric with the writer—not the grade level. Thus, when a child scored a "0" on the Early Writers rubric, the teacher scored the paper *again* with the Emergent Writers rubric. In this way, teachers addressed what each child *could do,* rather than using a deficit model that emphasized what the child's writing *lacked.* Furthermore, teachers attained a more thorough understanding of each child's growth from the beginning to the end of the year.

Remember that the progression from one rubric level to another represents a remarkable achievement. As children move through the emergent level, they are demonstrating that they are learning to reproduce what they see around them, internalizing their culture as they are learning to write, and mastering a complex code. Their efforts should be recognized and celebrated.

This does not mean, however, that we should exploit the concept of development. Children should not be left to play and experiment endlessly. They will not become competent writers simply through observing and practicing. Writing is a skill that must be learned through explicit, individualized, and purposeful instruction.

Keep in mind that development is intrinsically linked to environmental exposure, meaning that even a highly intelligent child will not master writing skills if she has not been exposed to literary behavior. When you look at a child's development as a writer in this light, it is easy to see how important it is for teachers to provide rich and rigorous literacy opportunities for children from low-literacy homes in order to fill the gaps and bring them up to the level of their peers. When we do, we see that by the end of kindergarten, most children will achieve a "5" on the emergent rubric, and, therefore, progress from emergent writers to early writers.

Progress to the Next Level

Progress from one level to the next depends on each child. In general, the first two levels of the emergent rubric are connected to muscle development and visual discrimination ability. Children who are scribbling and beginning to attempt letter formation still need a lot of time to explore with paper and pencil. They are, as my friend and colleague Jane Patrick describes, still "playing with the materials."

Explicit instruction of skills at the early writing stage should not occur until the child understands and masters the emergent skill set. All children should be exposed, however, to competent writing. Some children will soar through one level after another, assimilating and internalizing the rules of writing, while others will need instruction at each level.

Most important, remember that you *are* teaching these youngest writers critical pre-writing skills by developing their oral and listening abilities and their speaking vocabularies.

Early Writers Rubrics

Once a child achieves all the requirements of Level 5 of the Emergent Writer Rubric, we can introduce the remaining categories for analyzing writing. From Level 5 on, children write in complete sentences, and they are ready to learn about all the characteristics required to create meaningful pieces of writing. When children reach this level, they move from the category of Emergent Writers to the category of Early Writers.

Early Writers generally progress through content skills in the sequence below, grouped by the categories of *Attention to Audience, Expression of Language, Ideas,* and *Organization* to reflect the developmental sequence in which they tend to occur. A separate explanation of conventions and rubric for Understanding Conventions begins on page 35. I recommend assessing conventions separately at the Early Writers stage.

Attention to Audience

- First, second, or third person pronouns are used with inconsistencies.
- First, second, or third person pronouns are used in a consistent way.
- Readers do not "hear" the writer's unique voice or style of "speaking."
- Readers can "hear" the writer's unique voice and expression.

Expression of Language

- Sentences have a repetitive structure ("I like…").
- Sentences have a variety of structures.
- Sentences include descriptive words, such as verbs, adjectives, and adverbs.

Ideas

- Ideas are expressed in several **unrelated** sentences.
- Ideas are expressed in several **related** sentences and are joined by a **common theme.**

Organization

- Lack of organization among sentences and ideas.
- Organization of sentences includes an overall plan. (Supporting statements following each main point, for example.)
- Organization begins with an opening, or lead, sentence.
- Organization ends with a concluding sentence.

Unlike emergent writers, who are just beginning to understand what writing is and how to transpose the spoken word into print, early writers are able to focus on the details that comprise good writing. They are beginning to think about craft issues relating to content, such as which words to choose, how to begin a sentence, and how to describe a feeling or event. They also are trying to remember conventions, such as how to spell the words they have chosen, when to use a capital letter, where to put a period, and how to structure the syntax of their varied sentences.

In many cases, children attend to one or the other—content craft skills or conventions—at any given time. Each child receives, therefore, two scores on the same scale on the two rubrics: three being the highest, and one being the lowest.

As I determined with the Emergent Rubric, I determined the criteria for the Early Rubrics for Content and Early Rubric for Conventions by analyzing hundreds of writing samples each year and identifying how young writers develop competence in each of the writer's craft categories. The goal I suggest is to see children at the end of first grade achieving a score of "2" on each rubric and children at the end of second grade achieving a score of "3" on the same two rubrics.

Score	Characteristics
3	Addressing the Audience: The writer explains feelings, actions, and events, "speaking" in his unique voice for his audience. The writer uses first, second, or third person pronouns correctly. Expression of Language: All sentences are complete. The writer uses a variety of phrases and sentence structures, specific nouns, strong verbs, and sensory details. Ideas: All sentences relate to the same topic and include strong, well-developed supporting statements. Organization: The writer connects, sequences, and orders ideas in a logical way and includes an opening and an ending sentence.
2	Addressing the Audience: The writer explains most feelings, actions, and events, by "speaking" in his unique voice to his audience. The writer uses first-, second-, or third-person pronouns with few errors. Expression of Language: All sentences are complete. The writer uses two of the following: a variety of phrases and sentence structures, specific nouns, strong verbs, and sensory details. Ideas: All sentences relate to the same topic with some supporting statements._ Organization: The writer connects, sequences, and orders ideas in a logical way and includes either an opening or a closing sentence.
1	Addressing the Audience: The writer explains one feeling, action, or event without the presence of a unique voice. The writer uses first-, second-, or third-person pronouns with few or no errors. Expression of Language: The writer uses one complete sentence and may include one of the following: specific nouns, strong verbs, and sensory details. Ideas: The writer includes at least one complete sentence with no supporting statements. Organization: The writer connects, sequences, and orders one idea in a logical way but has no opening or closing sentence.
0	Addressing the Audience: The writer does not explain any feeling, action, or event. Expression of language: The writer does not use a complete sentence. Ideas: The writer does not express a complete idea. Organization: The writer does not connect, sequence, or order any idea in a logical way.

(If a child's writing scores a 0, score again with the Emergent Writer Rubric).

Score	Characteristics
3	**Capitalization:** All sentences begin with a capital letter. Few capitalization errors within sentences. (Proper nouns, "I," days of the week, and names of the months). **Punctuation:** All sentences have correct ending punctuation, including periods, question marks, and exclamation marks. Few errors (quotation marks and contractions) within sentences. **Spelling:** Few spelling errors of the 100 high-frequency words. **Grammar:** Few grammatical errors.
2	**Capitalization:** Most sentences begin with a capital letter. Some capitalization errors within sentences (e.g., Proper nouns, "I"). **Punctuation:** Most sentences have correct ending punctuation. Some punctuation errors (quotation marks and contractions) within sentences. **Spelling:** Some spelling errors of the 100 high-frequency words. **Grammar:** Some grammatical errors.
1	**Capitalization:** At least one sentence begins with a capital letter. Many capitalization errors within sentences (e.g., Proper nouns, "I"). **Punctuation:** At least one sentence has correct ending punctuation. **Spelling:** Many spelling errors of the 100 high frequency words. **Grammar:** Many grammatical errors.
0	No complete sentence

(Score again with emergent writer rubric)

Scoring

When a teacher scores her own students' papers, she learns a great deal about their ability to write independently. Teachers who support their children a great deal during class are often surprised by how ineffectively their students may perform on prompts written independently.

This insight is important for teachers, who tend to want to help their students as much as they can. Nonetheless, if we are going to determine how well students understand writing and measure their abilities to apply the writing skills we have taught, we need a snapshot of their independent work.

After the classroom teacher has assigned scores, the second scorer then looks at their papers and scores them again. The same scoring tool should be used to provide consistency in approach and scoring criteria for a particular paper. Discrepancies between the scorers offer an opportunity to discuss the papers and come to a consensus, which builds a common, school-wide understanding of writing levels.

In this scoring system, both scorers should be highly invested in the children doing well. The classroom teacher wants to see her students write well to reflect well on her teaching. The second scorer could be a staff member dedicated to the success of school's writing program. The second scorer should score all of the school's writing samples. A blank score sheet (Chart 2.1) can be found at the end of this chapter on page 48.

Determining the Score

The rubrics serve as a guide for getting a general sense of a child's writing level. Children do not always achieve *all* the criteria for any given score, but in my experience, they usually fit clearly into one of the levels. For example, a child may have one misplaced sentence, thus, showing some lapse in organization, yet the child may still receive a "3" on the rubric. If all the other criteria have been met and the child has written a substantial amount, the one lapse in organization need not shift the entire score.

Sample Analyses

As you score children's papers, you must be clear about what you are looking for. Alone, the rubrics mean very little. It is only in *how you apply them* towards actual writing samples that they generate information about students' individual writing needs. One helpful way to analyze a writing sample is to use the blank Chart 2.2 on page 49.

Next to a writing characteristic, you can document examples of how the child has demonstrated the ability to use it. The following three examples were responses to the prompt that asked children to tell about a day at school that they liked best. Each paper received a score of '3' for Content and a '3' for Conventions. After each sample, I have completed a chart to show how I determined the scores.

Our Trip to Oak View

Our trip to Oak View was fun because we went all around the school. It was fun because we got bookmarks. We even got to get cookies and juice. It's a big school. I liked the gym because it was big and it had basketball hoops. I met new teachers and students. I want Miss. Green to pick me as her student. I can't wait until I am in 3rd grade because I wan't harder homework. I like the playground because it has a soccer field. I can't wait until I am in 3rd grade.

Analysis of Writer's Craft — Completed Chart 2.2

Name: _____

Writing Sample: ____ "Our Trip to Oak View" ____

Craft Characteristics	Examples
"A" - Addressing your Audience	I can't wait I want Consistent use of first person
"E" - Expression of Language	We Even.. Variety of sentence lengths
"I" - Ideas	Main idea (Trip to Oak View) Many details (bookmarks, cookies and juice, gym, teachers and students, playground, soccer field)
"O" - Organization	Opening sentence Ending sentence Logical ordering of sentences
"U" - Understanding Conventions	Correct capitalization Correct punctuation Correct spelling Correct grammar

The Planetarium

The Planitarim

Yesterdaday I went on a field trip
to the planitarim. I had so much
fun! It was fun because we lea
learned about space! First we
were just looking at stars then
we saw pitchers and we saw marshens
in a sauser as a joke ha ha ha!
We also learned about natcher!
At the very end we saw horses!
And that was my field trip!
     The end
P.S We also learned about
constelatshins. We herd a story.

Name: _____

Writing Sample: _____"The Planitarim"_____

Craft Characteristics	Examples
"A" - Addressing your Audience	Voice: I had so much fun! Ha ha ha! Consistent use of the first person (I, we)
"E" - Expression of Language	So much fun First.. We also.. At the very end..
"I" - Ideas	Main topic (The planetarium) Many details (learning about space, stars, martians, nature, horses.)
"O" - Organization	Yesterday I went..(opening) And that was...(closing) Sentences ordered logically
"U" - Understanding Conventions	Capitalization correct Periods correct Use of exclamation marks Most spelling correct Grammar correct

Butterflies

I liked the day we let the
butterflys go. Our class rased
Panted Lady Caterpillars. After
they turned into butterflys we
let go free in nature. When
some flew out of the cage,
we said a pome. When we were
finished a few butterflys
were still in the cage. My
teacher had to help them
fly out. Unfortunately a bird
chased one of the butterfly
and had it for lunch. I felt sad
for the butterfly but I new
it was naturure. We woched
the butterfly for a while
then our class said the
pome agan and went inside.
that was really fun day for
me. I was really happy.

Name: _____

Writing Sample: _____"Butterflies"_____

Craft Characteristics	Examples
"A" - Addressing your Audience	Voice: I liked, I felt sad, a fun day for me, I was really happy. Consistent use of first person
"E" - Expression of Language	Free in nature After Unfortunately
"I" - Ideas	Main topic (letting butterflies go) Many details (raised them, let them free, poem, teacher help, bird, feelings)
"O" - Organization	I liked the day ..(opening) ..fun day ...I was really happy (closing) Sentences ordered logically
"U" - Understanding Conventions	Capitalization correct Periods correct Most spelling correct Grammar correct

All the above responses to prompts received the highest scores. As well as speaking to the audience in a strong voice, these pieces are well organized, detailed, and contain a variety of sentence patterns and descriptive words that make the writing flow well. While there are some spelling errors, the high-frequency words, as well as most of the other words, are spelled correctly. The words that do have spelling errors are not words we expect first or second graders to know.

The next group of writing samples received a score of 2 on the Content Rubric. They involve some organization and provide some information on the topic without including an expressive voice, a variety of sentence structures, or descriptive language. Of the three samples, the first one received a 3 on the Conventions Rubric, and the last two received a 2 on conventions.

Cheetahs

Chetes   1/18/02

Chetes run reale fast and eat
meat. Most ~~of~~ Chetes live in
Afirica. Chetes have sharp ~~x~~ teeth
They have long tails~~x~~ and they
have short legs. and

2/3

Analysis of Writer's Craft — Completed Chart 2.2

Name: _____

Writing Sample: ___"Chetes"_____

Craft Characteristics	Examples
"A" - Addressing your Audience	Written in third person No use of voice evident
"E" - Expression of Language	Complete sentences Adverb: "reale fast" Adjectives: sharp, long, short Repetitive sentence structure
"I" - Ideas	Main idea: Cheetahs Six details
"O" - Organization	Sentence organized by subtopic: Cheetah behavior, habitat, physical appearance No opening or closing sentence
"U" - Understanding Conventions	Correct use of capitals Correct use of periods Correct spelling Correct grammar

Dolphins

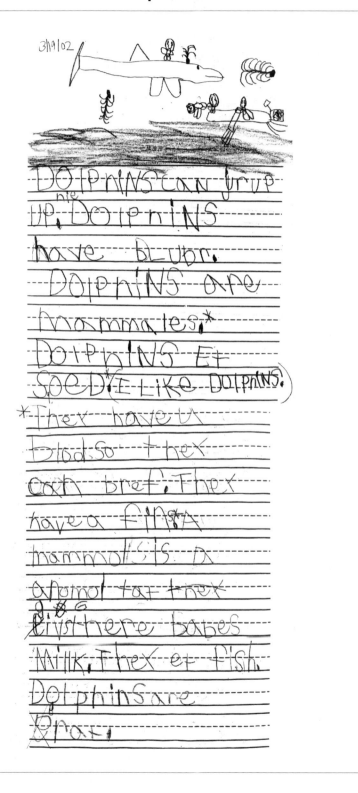

3/9/02

DOlPhINS can Jrup
UP. DOlPhINS
have BLubr.
DOlPhiNS are
mammales.*
DOlPhiNS et
soeD. I Like DOlPhiNS.

* They have ti
blodso they
can bref. They
have a fin A
mammol sis a
anomol tat they
feed there babes
Milk. They et fish.
Dolphins are
gray.

Name: _____

Writing Sample: "Dolphins"

Craft Characteristics	Examples
"A" - Addressing your Audience	Written in third person, with one inconsistency (I like dolphins)
"E" - Expression of Language	Complete sentences Adverb: "jump up" Adjectives: "Dolphins are great"
"I" - Ideas	Main idea: Dolphin facts Nine details
"O" - Organization	Sentence about mammals organized with revision technique of using a star. No opening sentence Closing: "Dolphins are great"
"U" - Understanding Conventions	Incorrect use of capitals (DolphiNs, caN) Correct use of periods Correct spelling of high frequency words Mostly correct grammar

Children who write at least one complete sentence on the topic receive a score of 1 on the Content Rubric. These papers generally state one idea without any supporting details and without much expression or voice communicated to the audience. Although the writing is brief, it is ordered and it makes sense to the reader. One example of a paper that was scored with a 1 on content is shown on page 45.

For conventions, the paper received a 1. (A paper with only one sentence cannot score higher than a "1" because enough material to determine whether the child understands that **every** sentence should begin with a capital and end with a period is unavailable.)

Snow

I see sonw on the heros.

Name: _____

Writing Sample: ____"Snow"_____

Craft Characteristics	Examples
"A" - Addressing your Audience	No evidence of voice. No explanation of feelings, actions, or events.
"E" - Expression of Language	One complete sentence.
"I" - Ideas	Main idea: Snow on the house. No supporting details.
"O" - Organization	Logical sentence.
"U" - Understanding Conventions	Capital letter at beginning. Period at the end. Correct grammar. High frequency words spelled correctly.

Weekly Writing Samples as a Supplement to Formal Assessments

Even with the best prompts, a formal writing assessment of a young child must be examined within the context of writing produced every day. As early childhood educators, we know that our young students are, after all, children first and react to the circumstances of their day, which may enhance or detract from their performance. A child who is hungry or who has a stomachache, for example, might not present his best writing on the day of the prompt.

By collecting weekly or bi-weekly samples of work done independently by each student, you can examine the responses to the school-wide prompts in relation to other work samples. Keep them in the same notebook in which you store the responses to the prompts. These samples become additional pieces of evidence to evaluate writing performance. The writing notebooks allow teachers to track their students' growth. One teacher explains, "I would look at the writing notebook every two weeks. It was amazing to me!"

That teacher also used the writing notebook to share the children's progress with them. "It was helpful to show the kids, and tell them, 'This was you three months ago.' They were able to recognize their own growth."

An easy way to collect writing samples is to mark the date on a piece of writing that the child does in his writing journal and then make a copy of it for the notebook at another time. Alternatively, keep a piece of dated writing from one of the writing-goal lessons, explained in Chapter 5. My colleague Jen Williams found that the requirement of collecting writing samples became a great help in her teaching. "I got in the habit of looking at their work and using sticky notes to mark the skills that they still needed to learn."

The notebooks also give teachers an organized and authentic system to present to parents and administrators. The notebooks become a helpful resource for parent conferences and for evaluation meetings with the school principal. In today's educational climate, we cannot underestimate the importance of school accountability.

Sharing Rubric Scores

Should rubric scores be shared with children? In a word, no. PreK-2 children are still learning the very basic concepts of expressing words on paper, and of reading. Exposing them to a written rubric before they begin to write with confidence or even understand all of the writing concepts in a rubric can confuse and inhibit them from freely expressing themselves.

While all children can learn and show improvement throughout the year, their learning needs to be individualized so that they can all feel successful. By holding them all to the same standards at the same time, you will be ensuring the success of some and the sense of frustration and failure of others. Interestingly, many of the finest classroom teachers who have written books on instruction and assessment for preK-2 children do not refer to rubrics at all.

Rubric scores are a tool for *teachers*. As useful as rubrics are for gathering data about progress and supplying a consistent way to measure a class, the numerical scores should *not* be shared with students before third grade. Quantitative assessments are either meaningless or damaging to a young child's efforts. Many children, especially English Language Learners, will not be able to achieve higher than a 0 or a 1. Other children will easily achieve a 2 or a 3 due to their background knowledge or their natural affinity for writing.

While the rubrics should not be *shown* to preK-2 children, the youngest writers *do* need feedback about their writing, and they do need to know how to improve their work. Feedback should focus on their efforts and should address the specific skills they should master next. Your comments—and focused explicit instruction—encourage the child to move towards the next skill.

Identifying specific skills to teach helps you develop a one-on-one, individualized approach, one that enables children to assess their own writing and work toward reaching their own writing goals. As Sharon Taberski writes in her book, *On Common Ground*, "The goals I set for each child depend on where he is on the developmental continuum and where he needs to go next." Carol Avery, in the book, *And with a Light Touch*, writes, "Examine the growth of the individual. Set goals with students but be flexible. Remember, growth may go in unpredictable directions."

Instead of showing young writers their rubric scores, share the individualized writing goals. The individualized writing goals let children know what they must do to improve their work. The goals simply present the essence of a rubric in a way that is easier for very young children to understand, and it leaves no room for child-to-child competition or comparisons. Setting those individual writing goals is the subject of the next chapter.

Names	Fall		Winter		Spring	
	Scorer 1	Scorer 2	Scorer 1	Scorer 2	Scorer 1	Scorer 2

* For emergent writers, record scores as E1, E2, E3, E4, or E5
* For early writers, record content score over conventions score, e.g. 2/1

Name: _____

Writing Sample: _____

Craft Characteristics	Examples
"A" - Addressing your Audience	
"E" - Expression of Language	
"I" - Ideas	
"O" - Organization	
"U" - Understanding Conventions	

Setting and Teaching Individual Writing Goals

How much to teach and what to expect often create a dilemma that clouds the real issue that we teachers face: what is the next instructional step for young writers? For example, what do we do with a first grader who is writing rows of letters? Or a second grader who writes a series of unrelated sentences as a narrative list? Teachers express frustration on both sides of this issue—from those who worry that we are expecting too much of our young writers to those who worry that their writing performance will not meet testing expectations.

My feeling, however, is that we sometimes do not know how to proceed— what we should do to move the child's writing forward. How do we know what the child is ready to learn *next*? Armed with the assessment tools that help you identify a child's current writing level, this chapter outlines strategies to define the "what comes next" writing goals that will move a young writer to the next level.

The Importance of Individual Writing Goals

Of course, we regard our class as a group in order to build a sense of community. American classrooms today, though, reflect enormous diversity, so much so that teachers must strive to understand the needs of each individual child. When it comes to teaching, we can no longer approach a classroom of children as a homogeneous group and expect that all students will learn if we simply follow the grade-level curriculum. Individual assessments help us plan instruction and analyze what those assessments imply for each child's instructional needs. When we individualize instruction, children learn and progress on their journeys to becoming competent writers. Cause for celebration results.

Determining Writing Goals for Each Child

The two series of writing goals below correspond to the criteria described in the Chapter 2 rubrics. The two basic **emergent writing goals** focus on the Emergent Writer Rubric, while the **early writing goals** are addressed in the Content Rubric for Early Writers and the Convention Rubric for Early Writers. Each series is arranged in an order that reflects the evolution of the development of a child's writing abilities. Noted in parentheses is the *approximate* time frame at which some children can be expected to attain the goals in each rubric. That said, remember that the curriculum should match whatever children are ready to learn and should not simply apply to grade levels. The point of these goals is to match the actual writing goals with the writing competency of the child—no matter *when* that actually happens.

Emergent Writing Goals (Kindergarten to Mid-Year First Grade)

To convey *"I", Ideas*, the student will:

- Scribble
- Draw a picture
- Write a word
- Write a phrase
- Write a complete sentence

To convey *"U," Understanding Conventions*, the student will:

- Write emergent letters
- Write conventional letters
- Write from left to right
- Write more than one line
- Use return sweep
- Use "sound spelling"
- Use conventional spelling
- Leave spaces between words
- Use a capital letter at the beginning of a sentence
- Put a period at the end of a sentence

Early Writing Goals (Mid-Year First Grade through Second Grade)

To convey *"A," Addressing Your Audience,* the student will:
- Write reflecting his unique voice
- Engage the reader with questions and other direct communication
- Use first-, second-, and third-person pronouns correctly and consistently

To convey *"E," Expression of Language,* the student will:
- Use complete sentences
- Use a variety of sentence lengths
- Use a variety of sentence structures
- Use sensory details, such as adjectives and adverbs
- Use a variety of verbs

To convey *"I," Ideas,* the student will:
- Choose a meaningful topic
- Develop ideas with details

To convey *"O," Organization,* the student will:
- Order sentences in a logical way
- Begin with an opening sentence
- End with a concluding sentence

To convey *"U," Understanding Conventions,* the student will:
- Begin sentences with a capital letter
- Use capitals for the word "I" and for proper nouns
- Use lower case letters in the middle of words
- End every sentence with a period
- Correctly use question marks
- Correctly use exclamation marks
- Correctly use quotation marks
- Use an apostrophe for contractions
- Use an apostrophe for possessive nouns
- Correctly spell high-frequency words
- Use sound spelling
- Use knowledge of spelling patterns
- Demonstrate subject-verb agreement
- Maintain past, present, or future tense
- Use the past, present, and future tenses correctly

After using the rubrics to analyze the writing of each child, a teacher then can select one writing goal in each category that addresses writing content (A, E ,I, and O) and one or two writing goals that address conventions (U). The basic rule of thumb is to work on moving children toward the next step in each writing goal category with a specific, explicit, and modeled mini-lesson, such as those that are discussed more fully in Chapter Five. For children who have already scored the top score of 3, continue improving the skills they already have.

You can use the Writing Goal Sheets at the end of this chapter (Charts 3.1, 3.2, 3.3, pages 59, 60, 61) to document the mini-lessons that you will use to move that child to the next step. Circle the writing goals selected for a particular child. Then use the column marked "Lessons" and list the lessons you will model to help the children reach their target writing goals.

You can create your own mini-lessons or begin by using those detailed in Chapter 5. Keep in mind that any writing goal can become a specific mini-lesson that teaches a new skill. The important concept to remember is that you will explicitly teach each skill first. Throughout the year, use your judgment to identify new goals. If a child is reaching his goals easily, then clearly he is ready for more. Another child who may be struggling should be given perhaps fewer skills to address at one time.

Writing Goals and ELL Children

Young, native English speakers can begin to consider writer's craft issues, such as choosing which word best describes what they are trying to say or applying inverted sentence structure to form a question without effort. However, young ELL children must first learn the words, what they mean, and how to use them. Of course, as they learn the words, they can also learn how to write them down, but their application of craft in writing takes a little more time to develop. As ELL children develop their English speaking skills, more writing goals should be expected.

An interesting parallel exists between the language stages that Paton Tabors describes in her book, *One Child, Two Languages,* and the appearance of craft characteristics in the young child. Children can work toward writing goals that complement each of the stages identified by Tabors. The language stages and selected, parallel writing goals follow:

Home-language use, non-verbal period → drawing pictures to convey ideas

Writing serves as a very useful vehicle during the initial step, during which the child uses his home language and non-verbally begins to acquire a second language. As the young ELL student draws pictures during writing workshop, her teacher can use those pictures to try to voice her thoughts and to provide the English words for them.

For example, a Spanish-speaking first grader might draw flowers, grass, and a sun, not knowing the English words for the objects. Her teacher can point to the sun, for example, and say, "sun," thus validating the child's work while providing her with an English word. Once the English word is identified, the teacher can then help the child connect the sounds heard in the word to the corresponding letters, using the same strategy used with English speakers.

By using a child's own drawing as a foundation for teaching English vocabulary, the teacher is employing the theory of "comprehensible input." This phrase, initially coined by Jim Cummins (1979), means that a person must have some level of understanding and support while learning a new language. When a child's picture serves as a springboard for language, the association she makes between her drawing and the new words helps her to learn, understand, and remember them.

Telegraphic speech and formulaic speech → developing word choice

As ELL children enter this stage, they have a repertoire of single words to label objects and ideas. Teachers can encourage them to write those words next to their pictures. A child may, for example, write "sn" or the word "sun," which the teacher could project into the sentence, "The sun is yellow," by using the child's picture.

As they learn formulaic speech, they begin to use common words and phrases, such as "OK," "hi," "bye-bye," and "look here." Again, teachers can encourage children to write those words with their pictures.

Productive language use → developing grammatically correct complete sentences

In this stage of language acquisition, a child's writing will reflect her developing verbal skills and will provide opportunities for the teacher to build on her growing mastery of the language.

At this point, ELL children can learn English grammar and vocabulary through writing. For example, a child in the productive stage might write,

"I go school" for "I go to school" or "He not friend" for "He is not my friend." Just as you can help a child develop his speech during an oral exchange, you can also praise his writing and his idea, and then you can help him by providing the correct English syntax. Again, explaining orally how to construct the sentence grammatically is the same strategy used with English speakers. There is no shame or criticism, simply an opportunity for instruction, which for ELL children supports the development of their English skills while also addressing specific writing skills.

Writing instruction that emphasizes expressing ideas orally allows you to guide the children through the different stages of language acquisition, and, thus, provide reciprocal support to the oral practice commonly used in ELL instruction. Moreover, because children's writing is a reflection of their language abilities at that moment in time, their writing gives you insight into and documents the stages of English acquisition.

Grouping Children

After the children have been assigned their specific writing skills, you can group those at the same level for lessons that address their needs. **I am not proposing, however, that children be permanently grouped according to overall ability.** One child may be with three others for a lesson on spelling high-frequency words and then with five different children for a lesson on organizing information. See the checklist grids (Charts 3.4 and 3.5) at the end of this chapter on pages 62 and 63 to help you keep track of which children are working on which skills. By writing the children's names down the left side and putting a check mark in the columns of the appropriate skill lessons, you can easily analyze which skills can be assigned to all children and which should be assigned to just a few. You can refer to this grid when planning lessons and calling the children together.

The rubric scores and the writing goals are both useful and important. Rubric scores give an overall picture of the progress of a child, a class, a grade level, and a school. While we should analyze the overall status of each class and of each school, our main focus should remain on charting individual learning and helping each child progress with specific writing skills. Individual writing goals are the means to achieve that end.

When you assess your own students' needs—collaboratively setting goals with each child to help improve writing and then delivering carefully selected lessons that address those goals—you can formulate a clear plan to follow and understand what to teach and to whom. When my colleague Jen Williams sought my help with some of her students, for example, she was able to articulate their needs and their goals clearly. In an e-mail to me she wrote:

"Hi, Melissa. Here are the names of kids who I feel would benefit from small group instruction. Diana—she has difficulty organizing her thoughts in a logical order and works very slowly. Bao—he has good ideas but he needs someone to help him focus and get the ideas in writing. Both children have spelling as a writing goal as well as basic language issues."

Sharing Writing Goals with Students

Individual writing goals are functionally equivalent to rubrics but are better suited for preK-2 children to see and to use. Writing goals are concrete, matching the intellectual abilities of young children, while rubrics are abstract and beyond a young child's ability to understand. Rubrics also focus on several criteria at once, which may overwhelm and discourage a young child. A writing goal, however, focuses on only one criterion at a time.

Children should know their writing goals so that they can work toward meeting them. Knowing the goals also invites them to share in the responsibility for their own learning, thus empowering them as learners. The task of writing seems less daunting and becomes a manageable task with clear expectations.

Once you have selected writing goals for each student, sit down with each child and explain them. The process helps both you and your student. As Gabrielle Schechter, an ELL teacher, shared with me, "The goals helped organize me. I knew what the focus was for each child. They also helped the kids when I sat down and explained them. As they began to meet their goals, for example, putting in periods, I showed them that they were doing it and we moved to the next goal."

Jen Williams sat down with each of her students, commented on which goals they had achieved, and then said, "I looked at your writing. This is what you need to work on," and then explained the next writing goal. While children move along the continuum of writing development by learning a progressive set of skills, the conversations and explorations of their ideas with the teacher remain an important foundation for learning. The manner in which the teacher explains the writing goals and shows the child the reason for those goals is critical to the child's progress.

Writing Goals Presented in "Children's Words"

This next list simply rewrites the writing goals explained previously in the first person, in language that children understand. These personalized goals create a sense of ownership in the young writer.

My Writing Goals

"A" - Addressing your Audience

I will write about my feelings and things I did.
I will write the same words that I speak so that my readers hear my voice.
I will ask my readers questions and speak right to them.
I will think about my readers as I use the words, "I," "we," "you," "he," "she," and "they."

"E" - Expression of Language

I will write sentences that tell whole ideas.
I will choose wonderful describing words that make pictures in my readers' minds.
I will choose wonderful action words that make pictures in my readers' minds.
I will write sentences that begin in different ways.
I will write short sentences and long sentences.

"I" - Ideas

I will choose to write about something that I think about and care about.
I will explain everything I write by telling at least three things about each idea.

"O" - Organization

I will put sentences together that tell about the same idea.
I will write an opening sentence.
I will write an ending sentence.

"U" - Understanding Conventions

<u>Capitals</u>

I will begin every sentence with a capital letter.
I will use a capital letter for the word "I" and for a person's name.
I will use lower-case letters in the middle of words.

<u>Punctuation</u>

I will put a period at the end of every sentence.
I will put a question mark at the end of a sentence that asks a question.
I will put an exclamation mark at the end of a sentence that tells that I am excited.
I will use quotation marks to show when someone is talking.

I will use an apostrophe when I write a contraction.
I will use an apostrophe when I use a possessive noun.

Spelling

I will write the words on the word wall the way they are spelled.
I will listen to the sounds as I say a word slowly, and I will write down the letters I hear.
I will listen to the sounds as I say a word slowly, and I will write down the spelling patterns I hear.

Grammar

I will use the words "I," "we," "you," "he," "she," and "they" correctly.
I will think about when the actions happen so that my readers know if they were in the past, are happening now, or if they will happen in the future.

Visual Reminders of Writing Goals for Emergent Readers

Visual reminders, such as icons, are helpful for emergent readers. Some teachers choose to glue the writing skills in the front of each child's writing notebook, while others display them on the children's tables or desks. Whatever system is used, children need to know what their individual writing goals are and to be reminded of them every time they write. As one first-grade teacher explains, "The writing goals make the children more aware of what they are supposed to do as they write." See the chart of visual writing goals at the end of this chapter on pages 64-65 (Chart 3.6).

When Do Children Learn to Apply Their Writing Goals?

Each writing goal and the skill mini-lessons that the teacher develops and models can be matched to a step in the writing process. This helps children to remember when they should apply that skill. For example, writing goals that address *"I," Ideas,* such as how to choose a topic, apply to the first and second steps in the writing process: prewriting and writing a rough draft. Writing goals that address *"A," Addressing Your Audience,* and *"E," Expression of Language,* such as varying sentences, apply to the third step in the process: revising the rough draft. Those that deal with *"U," Understanding Conventions,* such as punctuation, spelling, and capitalization, apply to the fourth step: editing.

By addressing the various steps of writing in a sequential manner, children attend to one writing goal at a time, rather than becoming overwhelmed with the many aspects of writing. For each goal attempted, a step in the writing process offers an opportunity to apply it.

Child's Name/Grade _____   Target Date: _____

Teacher's Name _____

Writing Goals	Lessons to Use
"I" Ideas	
Will scribble	
Will draw a picture	
Will write a word (e.g., "name")	
Will write a phrase (e.g., "My mom")	
Will write a sentence	
"U" Understanding Conventions	
Will scribble	
Will write emergent letters	
Will write conventional letters	
Will write from left to right	
Will write more than one line	
Will use sound spelling	
Will use conventional spelling	
Will leave spaces between words	
Will begin sentences with a capital	
Will end sentences with a period	

Child's Name/Grade _____   Target Date: _____

Teacher's Name _____

Writing Goals	Lessons to Use
"A" Addressing your Audience	
Will explain actions, feelings, events	
Will write in unique voice	
Will correctly use 1st, 2nd, 3rd person	
"E" Expression of Language	
Will use complete sentences	
Will use a variety of sentence lengths	
Will use a variety of sentence structures	
Will use adjectives and adverbs	
Will use a variety of verbs	
"I" Ideas	
Will choose a meaningful topic	
Will develop ideas with details	
"O" Organization	
Will order sentences in a logical way	
Will begin with an opening sentence	
Will end with a concluding sentence	

Child's Name/Grade _____   Target Date: _____

Teacher's Name _____

Writing Goals	Lessons to Use
"U" Understanding Conventions	
Will begin sentences with a capital	
Will use capital for "I" and proper nouns	
Will use lower case in middle of words	
Will end every sentence with a period	
Will correctly use questions marks	
Will correctly use exclamation marks	
Will correctly use quotation marks	
Will use an apostrophe for contractions	
Will use apostrophe for possessive nouns	
Will spell high-frequency words	
Will use sound spelling	
Will use spelling patterns	

Emergent Writing Goals Determined by Writing Prompt — Chart 3.4

"U" Understanding Conventions	Puts a period at the end of a sentence									
	Uses a capital at a beginning of a sentence									
	Leaves space between words									
	Uses conventional spelling									
	Uses sound spelling									
	Writes more than one line									
	Writes from left to right									
	Writes conventional letters									
	Writes emergent letters									
	Scribbles									
"I" Ideas	Writes a complete sentences									
	Writes a phrase									
	Writes a word									
	Draws pictures									
	Scribbles									
Names										

Early Writing Goals Determined by Writing Prompt — Chart 3.5

"U" **Understanding Conventions**	Uses spelling patterns					
	Uses sound spelling					
	Correctly spells high-frequency words					
	Uses an apostrophe for possessive nouns					
	Uses an apostrophe for contractions					
	Correctly uses quotation marks					
	Correctly uses exclamation marks					
	Correctly uses question marks					
	Ends every sentence with a period					
	Uses lowercase letters in the middle of words					
	Uses capitals for "I" and proper nouns					
	Begins sentences with a capital					
"O" **Organiza-tion**	Ends with a concluding sentence					
	Begins with an opening sentence					
	Orders sentences in a logical way					
"I" **Ideas**	Develops ideas with details					
	Chooses a meaningful topic					
"E" **Expression of Language**	Uses a variety of verbs					
	Uses adjectives and adverbs					
	Uses a variety of sentence structures					
	Uses a variety of sentence lengths					
	Uses complete sentences					
"A" **Addressing Your Audience**	Correctly uses 1st, 2nd, 3rd person					
	Writing reflects unique voice					
	Explains actions feelings events					
Names						

	I will write about my feelings and what I did.		I will write sentences that begin in different ways.
	I will write the same words that I speak using my own special voice.		I will write short and long sentences.
	I will use the words "I," "We," "You," "He," "She," and "They."		I will choose to write about something I think about and care about.
	I will write sentences that tell whole ideas.		I will put an exclamation mark after writing an idea that is exciting.
	I will write describing words that make pictures in my readers' minds.		I will use quotation marks to show that someone is talking.
	I will write action words that make pictures in my readers' minds.		I will use an apostrophe when I write a contraction.

My dog's nose.	I will use an apostrophe when I write a possessive noun.	ending	I will write an ending sentence.
My W.W.	I will write the words on the word wall the way they are spelled.	I Leo	I will use a capital letter for the word "I" and for the first letter in a person's name.
	I will listen to the sounds as I say a word slowly, and I will write the letters I hear.	.The	I will begin every sentence with a capital letter.
3	I will explain what I write by telling three things about my ideas.	like	I will use lower-case letters in the middle of words.
	I will put sentences together that tell about the same ideas.	•	I will put a period at the end of every sentence.
Opening	I will write an opening sentence.	?	I will put a question mark after writing a question.

Instructional Strategies

A little girl brings a note home from school every day, telling her mother that she loves her "so, so, so, so much." A five-year-old writes to his father, who lives across the country, asking him please to come and visit. A second grader writes to her teacher, who is mourning the death of her father, "I wish you peace and love."

By giving young children the opportunity to participate in genuine writing, we teach them to love writing. Writing is meaningful if we show children that the purpose for writing is to communicate on paper to others. For young children, learning must be purposeful and meaningful if we want them to engage in our lessons.

Making sure that our classrooms are rich with oral language and conversation, as discussed in Chapter 1, is surely the first and most important instructional strategy for teaching the youngest writers, but especially for Title I and ELL students. The instructional strategies in this chapter help create a classroom climate that promotes and supports purposeful and meaningful writing.

Strategy One: Begin Each School Day with a Class Meeting

My experiences teaching children in Head Start, kindergarten, and later in first and second grade have shown me that a daily class meeting is an excellent way to give students opportunities to find meaningful writing topics, to provide a forum for conversational practice, and to help them feel comfortable expressing their ideas aloud.

In addition, class meetings:

- create a warm, safe, and respectful classroom community;
- help children become aware of their world and how they perceive it;
- give them a place to discuss ideas and issues that are important to them;
- provide an opportunity for the teacher to ask open-ended questions that will help the young writers to develop writing topics;
- teach speaking and active listening skills;
- show children that their verbal ideas can be transferred into the written word.

A daily class meeting starts the instructional day. Before the children arrive, write your daily plan on a large flip chart. This allows them to know what you will be doing for the day and what you expect them to learn. A daily plan might say, for example, "During writer's workshop today, we will take out one of our pieces and pay attention to the words we have chosen. We will be careful to choose a word that will create a picture in a reader's mind."

As the children enter the classroom, they put away their belongings and sit in a circle near the chart, on a rug if you have one. As they wait for others to arrive, they can look at books that you make available in baskets nearby. Once most of the children have arrived, you can sing a favorite "Hello" song to begin the class meeting. (My favorite is "Say Hello," by children's recording artists Greg and Steve.)

After singing, read the daily plan aloud. Then ask the children a simple question, such as, "Who has something they would like to share?" From that question on, the agenda is simply to allow the children's interests to guide the conversation. I used my class meetings to listen very carefully to the students' ideas and the quality of their oral language and to monitor their levels of comfort and confidence.

Using open-ended questions to guide the flow of the conversation allows each child to talk about what is on his or her mind. Open-ended discussions, as opposed to the more traditional, teacher-directed, question-and-answer exchanges, engage students in higher-level thinking.

You can help them find connections between their comments. For example, "When Richard was telling us about how he takes care of his little sister, I remembered what Tania told us about being at her babysitter's house with her two baby cousins. Both Richard and Tania know what hard work it is to take care of babies!"

By modeling the process of making mental connections, you can demonstrate to the children how to think actively about what they are hearing—a skill that they need for listening comprehension, reading comprehension, and for writing as well. By modeling thinking in this way, you teach children to be active listeners and participants and members of an academic environment in which each person is treated with respect and dignity.

The tone of the class meeting conversation is important, and it will determine whether your young writers will volunteer to share their ideas or sit in intimidated silence. By focusing on the child who is speaking, you model listening skills for the others and create a sense of trust and safety for the speaker. When other children are inattentive, you can easily redirect them to the need to listen. You can say, for example, "I'm really trying to listen to Jose right now because he is saying something very important. It's hard for me to listen when you are talking."

You can maintain a similarly non-threatening tone when a child has difficulty formulating a thought, for example, "Do you need a few minutes to get your words ready?" or "Do you want to change your mind and tell about something else?"

By giving the children an opportunity to talk freely, you will learn a great deal about them. During my class meetings, I learned about their families and interests and their lives at home. Occasionally, there were sad days when the children told me about situations at home that led me to report my concern to the principal or the school counselor, but I was glad to have the information so I could help. For the most part, the conversations gave me a mental database about them that helped me guide my instruction. Because I knew which subjects excited them, I could help them discover topics for writing or bring in books that interested them.

Later, as the children write, you can emphasize the connection between talking and writing and the fact that all good writers get ideas by talking and listening to other people. For example, "I'm so glad you're writing about your cat. I was interested when you were talking about her, and now I'll get to read about her, too."

Gabrielle Schechter, a talented second-grade ELL teacher who has used the class-meeting approach to help her students develop writing ideas, explains, "I would rather take ten minutes away from writing and spend ten minutes talking to help a student find ideas for writing." Like so many teachers, Gabrielle has learned from experience that it is hard for the youngest students to write without talking first.

In my classroom, the daily meeting generally lasted from ten to fifteen minutes. At its conclusion, I would announce, "Whoever is ready to write may leave the meeting and return to their seat to begin writing."

Writing immediately after the class meeting—when the children's spoken words and the ideas they have reflected on conversationally in the class meeting are still fresh—is a predictable routine that the children anticipate. Use your own judgment, based on the children you teach, to decide how much time to spend writing. As a rule, I have kindergarten students write for about 20 minutes, first graders for about 30 minutes, and second graders from about 40 minutes to an hour. Just make sure that each child has found a meaningful topic for writing before he leaves the class meeting.

Benefits of Class Meeting to Second Language Learners

Because the class meeting is all about talking, it provides support for children at all levels of second language acquisition to practice English and to hear it spoken by teachers and peers. The class meeting gives teachers a valuable opportunity to monitor the development of their ELL students—at whatever level of development they have achieved.

As described in Chapter 3, Paton Tabors identifies the "home-language use" stage as the first level of learning a new language. At this level, children speak their home language at school, not realizing that most of the people around them do not understand what they are saying. A class meeting helps these children quickly see that the other members of the class do not respond to their ideas appropriately or understand the words they are speaking.

Children enter the "non-verbal" stage after they realize that those around them are speaking a language other than their own. They understand they must learn the new language, and they take time to try to figure it out before they try to speak it themselves. (During this stage, children may use gestures or facial expressions to convey ideas.) Class meetings give children many opportunities to listen to spoken English and to absorb words and phrases.

During this period of silent listening, you can expect that children will offer their ideas when they are more comfortable and willing to talk, i.e., after most of the other students have gone to their seats to begin writing. In fact, many teachers have told me that these moments were the first time that they heard these children speak at all. Other ELL children who choose not to speak during the class meeting will reassure you that they know what they are going to write. Although they are not ready to talk, they are able to generate ideas through listening, and they will respond by "drawing" the writing.

In the next stage, the "telegraphic speech" stage, children will often use one word at a time as they master it. They tend to label objects and to use basic-skills words, such as numbers and colors. Class meetings provide a safe forum for them to practice using the words they are learning.

As they enter the "formulaic speech" stage, children use phrases that they have heard before, replicating the phrases in similar situations to those in which they had initially heard the expressions used. For example, "I don't know." Again, class meetings give them a safe opportunity to practice.

Finally, as ELL children begin to combine words and phrases to construct their own sentences in the "productive speech" stage, class meetings offer an ideal place to share their ideas and increase their oral vocabularies. As they begin to put a few words together, we can respond enthusiastically, repeating their ideas to validate them and to model English usage. For example, if a child says, "I goed to the park. I play on slide," I might respond, "You went to the park and you played on the slide? Did you have a good time?"

The more opportunities we provide for our ELL students to speak, the more information we gain about the status of their language acquisition and what they need from us to do even better. Class meetings are the ideal venue for supporting them at their own levels.

Strategy Two: Monitoring the Instructional Tone

The most basic strategy you have is the way in which you speak to your students, particularly in the kinds of questions you ask and in the way you make suggestions for improvement. For example, when you say with no preamble, "You didn't use a capital letter at the beginning of your sentence," the statement does point out the child's mistake and implies she should remember to use capital letters. The comment, however, does not encourage the student to analyze the error or to work on the skill.

Consider the different outcome if you would say something like, "I notice that you are using lower case letters at the beginning of your sentences. Do you see where they are? When we read books, what kind of letters do you notice the authors using at the beginning of their sentences? Do you know why? What can you do to remember to use capital letters the next time you write?"

First, a child's current ability is noticed, praised, and validated, and then the teacher points to the next step. The positive tone promotes learning, helps the child make connections, and offers food for active thought.

Learn How to Ask Good Questions

As we help our students to explore their ideas, we need to be clear about what we are asking. If we simply ask them, "What happened next?" after they write a sentence or two, their output will be as empty and meaningless as our input. Children have a keen ability to perceive whether their teachers are truly interested in their thoughts or whether they are just trying to lead them to complete a task.

Very often, young writers do not provide enough details to explain their ideas. Asking students appropriate questions will help them discover the details they need to overcome this problem. Let them know you will ask questions, and prepare them for independence by telling them that after a lot of practice answering your questions, they should remember to ask *themselves* the same kinds of questions as *they* speak and as they write.

During your class time, use the following five types of questions that help your young writers to expand their ideas—either before or after they have chosen a topic. Use them during the class meeting or when you work with children independently.

- Ask the child for *clarification* ("Tell me who went with you to the doctor. I didn't hear that part right.")
- Ask the child to explain *how she felt*. ("How did you feel while you were waiting to see the doctor?")
- Ask the child to *speculate*. ("Why do you think you got sick? Do you think you caught some germs from someone else who was also sick?")
- Ask the child if his experience *reminds him of anything*. ("Do you remember anyone else telling us about a time when they were sick or when they went to the doctor?")

- Ask the child if his experience *reminds him of anything he read in a book before.* ("Can you think of a book we have read with a character who was sick?")

You pose these questions not to test the child's memory or to look for correct answers, but to help a student find the details he needs to develop his writing adequately. When you ask these questions sincerely, you show young writers that you are really listening to their ideas and that you are interested enough to want to hear more. You build their confidence in their abilities to write and stimulate more opportunities for conversation with other children.

How you ask the questions is even more important than what you ask. I suggest a tone that is interested, curious, and focused. Perhaps a child's story about going to a fast food restaurant does not actually intrigue you, but if you actively listen, you can respond with genuine interest. For example, you might try to remember the excitement you felt as a little girl going out to eat with your own family or wonder if the child's parents were so tired after working a hard day that they frequently would rather eat out than cook at home.

Whatever your thought associations, try to remember than if a child's anecdote is important enough to share with the class, it becomes a snapshot of his life. He should feel validated after he speaks. When he does, he will believe that the stories from his life are important enough to write about, and he will be less likely to stare at a piece of paper thinking that he has nothing of value to tell.

Strategy Three: Connecting Children's Lives to Books

In an essay entitled "The Having of Wonderful Ideas," Eleanor Duckworth talks about giving children time to "mess about" with materials before we ask them to do anything structured. She writes,

> Making new connections depends on knowing enough about something in the first place to provide a basis for thinking of other things to do—of other questions to ask—that demand more complex connections in order to make sense. The more ideas about something people already have at their disposal, the more new ideas occur and the more they can coordinate to build up still more complicated schemes. (14)

She summarizes this justification for students needing to "mess about" in what I believe to be a very poignant and notable statement: "Wonderful ideas do not spring out of nothing. They build on a foundation of other ideas" (6).

It makes sense to connect their experiences to powerful fiction and nonfiction literature that reflects their lives and presents similar scenarios in new ways. As they listen to a book about a topic they know something about, they have a basis for understanding and comprehending the new information. In essence, we choose books on topics on which children already have some background knowledge.

Each book is immediately meaningful and helps them make connections to their own lives. Wonderful books matched to the experiences of children give them fresh ideas and new perspectives on familiar things, broadening their perspectives on and providing insight into their own experiences.

After reading a book you have chosen, ask, "What did the book make you think of?" and begin a class conversation. Keep the conversation about the children's lives and the book authentic and personal, and try to find connections to the book from whatever a child has been sharing. I offer these points to consider as you talk with the students, to help them understand the meaning and relevance of the books to their lives. Ask them the following types of questions:

- Why did I choose this book? (What had we talked about?)
- How were the events/characters in the book similar to our experiences?
- How were they different?
- What other books did the book make us think about? (Read them next!)

Here is an example of a conversation with a group of first graders early in the academic year, written as they actually spoke. It happened that during a class meeting one child talked about the mice in her apartment, which prompted several other children to share similar stories. I used the opportunity to read them Don Freeman's book, *Norman the Doorman,* about a very special and talented mouse. I was interested to see their reaction to a mouse that was also considered a pest but who was actually a gifted artist and a kind creature!

The discussion about *Norman the Doorman* occurred before the children began to write a piece for their day's writing workshop, to help them discover a meaningful topic for their writing.

> **Melissa Landa (ML):** "I wanted to remind you why I chose this book for you. Do you remember?" (Question Type 1)
> **Rita:** "'Cause we talked about mice!"
> **ML:** "Who was the character in this book who was trying to catch

the mice? Who was it? Mary, do you remember?" (Question Type 2)

Maritza: "The mean man."

Victor: "The sharp-eyed guard!"

ML: "Wonderful! You remembered the exact words out of the book!" (The sharp-eyed guard). "Now, I have a question for you. Why was the sharp-eyed guard in the book trying to find the mouse?" (Question Type 2)

Luis: "To catch him."

ML: "Why was he trying to catch him?" (Question Type 2)

Victor: "He doesn't want a mouse in that place."

ML: "He doesn't want a mouse in that place. Is that sort of like you when you don't want mice in your family's apartment? Is that the same, Maria?" (Question Type 2)

Maria: "Yeah."

ML: "Why do you think people don't want mice in their apartments or in their museums? What can mice do that we don't like?" (Question Type 2)

John: "They can bite!"

Rita: "Break things."

Justin: "They're looking for cheese."

ML: "Yeah! They're looking for cheese, and they're going to eat *your* cheese. That's right!"

ML: "But what about Norman? Did Norman want to do all those bad things?" (Question Type 3)

All: "NO!"

Marvin: "Norman was an artist!"

Victor: "He just wanted to show everybody what he did as an artist, but the sharp-eyed guard, he wanted to let no mouse to come in. But the other man gave him an award and he just wanted never, ever to be catched again.

ML: "So he just wanted to go and see all the beautiful artwork in the museum. Now that we have talked about the book, about mice in our homes, and about Norman, if you feel like you have an idea right now and you're ready to go and write, you may do that. But if you'd like to stay on the rug and talk some more about the book, you can do that. Who feels like they're ready to go and do some writing and drawing?"

As your class converses in this way, complete Chart 4.1, found on page 88. Children then choose one of the ideas to write about. Remind them that good writers often get their topics from other authors' books. Tell them that whenever a book makes them think about something important to them, they should try to write about it. This strategy can lead to powerful and poignant writing, as the example below, written in response to the book *Tar Beach* illustrates.

5-25-99

My trip to hounduras

When I go to Hounduras I will go to the beach to see how it is in honduras. Maybe I'll swim for a while. I'll go when it's not because the water is cold and fresh and then I won't feel hot. I think it will be cool going to the beach because I'll get to swim and splash. I like splashing because it makes water go in my eye. I will also see my Grandma. I havent seen my grandma since october 4, 1998. She left because the law sent her. My mom kept telling her that she was supposed to go on september 1st 1998 but she didn't listen. I felt very sad. Almost all my family and cousins were crying and my grandma was too. I felt really sorry for her. She is going to come back in three months. I am exited because we will go to mcdomolds evry morning like we did when she used to be here. I always dream about her and that makes me feel even more exited We also will go to the park Walking quietly and talking about how it was in Hounduras and talking about how the beach felt. I am so happy that I am going to see her agen

Naturally, being able to respond to a child by referring to a book with a similar theme or with similar characters requires a familiarity with an extensive repertoire of children's literature. We are fortunate that today we can find hundreds of wonderful books written for children that deal with many aspects of their lives. Some of my favorites are in the Annotated

Bibliography on page 133. Grouped by topics such as Grandparents, Independence, or Pets, the selections include fiction and nonfiction. Each entry contains a brief summary with its theme or themes. Using powerful books like these as models leads to powerful writing.

Strategy Four: Making Class Books

Making a class book is one of the best ways to begin to teach children how to craft a strong piece of writing on their own. Largely created in a shared setting, a class book helps to introduce and teach the steps of the writing process, and it gives us a good opportunity to introduce elements of craft for children to practice in a highly supported way.

Class books can be shared with children as young as four years old in a Head Start classroom to expose them to the general concepts involved with writing a piece for publication. They can be used to introduce kindergartners to the techniques and steps in the writing process. With first and second graders, class books demonstrate the writing skills they are expected to apply independently as they write a rough draft, revise, and edit their own pieces for practice and publication.

All children who participate in creating the class book are *exposed* to the writing process and its accompanying terminology (pre-writing, drafting, revising, editing, publishing) and to the terminology of writing characteristics (ideas, elaboration, organization). The teacher demonstrates these terms so that the children eventually become familiar enough with the concepts to apply and incorporate them independently.

If taught in the way described below, class books can do more than teach children to draw a picture, write down their own words, and then staple all the pages together. This type of class book invites young writers to participate more fully in all the steps of the writing process as they think about how to craft the writing appropriate to their ages and developmental levels.

General Guidelines for Class Books

You show children the importance of writers' ideas when you select a topic for the class book. Allow them to select the topic by voting on suggestions or after discussing options until they reach agreement. Explain that good writers choose topics that they care about and that are interesting to them. Because the class book is a group effort, explain that the topic needs to be of shared interest. In my experience, favorite topics have included animals (class pets, sea creatures, and bats), the solar system, and different world cultures.

Children create the class book during writing workshop. Each step is modeled as a mini-lesson, followed by the children's independent writing and illustrating. Therefore, each step requires at least one day, and maybe more.

The teacher decides how often to create class books. If children need more modeling of the writing process, a second or third class book helps. If a new science or social studies unit begins, a class book creates excitement about the topic.

Benefits of Nonfiction Class Books

In the past few years, much excellent nonfiction literature for children has been published. Vivid writing and excellent photographs and illustrations will engage your young writers, who are naturally curious about the world around them. They can become powerful models for elements of good writing even as they demonstrate steps in the writing process itself.

Nonfiction literature also helps children learn important features of text not present in fiction. Children learn how to create indexes and glossaries and to understand the concepts of labels and captions, which they will add to their illustrations. These skills serve them well as writers and as readers. When they are later asked to respond to nonfiction text—either as part of the classroom-reading program or on a standardized test—children who have created their own books are familiar and comfortable with these features.

Nonfiction writing plays an especially significant role as ELL children learn English. As they write about topics such as planets or sea creatures, they learn to use the academic language that they will be expected to read in books and to use throughout their education. Through writing, they begin to incorporate academic words and concepts and increase their "Cognitive Academic Language Proficiency" (CALP), a term coined by Jim Cummins, a second-language acquisition researcher. As noted in Chapter 1, Cummins' research found that ELL children need *five to seven years* to acquire academic language, as opposed to needing only one to two years to acquire everyday, functional "Basic Interpersonal Communication Skills."

By pointing out the distinction between everyday and academic language, Cummins explains why so many ELL children read without comprehending, perform poorly on tests, and fall further and further behind their peers. Although they are able to speak English to their friends and can participate in play and conversation, they have not yet acquired the academic language found in books and on tests. Nonfiction class books give ELL children good exposure to academic ideas, and the process of writing the book together teaches ELL children the vocabulary and structure of the English language.

Making Class Books in Head Start or PreK

GOAL: Expose children to the general concepts involved with writing a piece for publication.

Step One: Have chart paper and markers ready to do a shared writing. Choose a topic of high interest to the children that all the children share. A good example is the classroom pet.

Step Two: Gather the children on the rug and tell them that they are going to make a book about their classroom pet. Ask each of them to tell you something about the pet. Point out that this is where the class "brainstorms" ideas, a part of the process of pre-writing. All ideas should be accepted.

Step Three: Write down the ideas of each child, followed by that child's name. For example: "The gerbil eats" - Giselle

If a child does not offer an idea, prompt her with questions. For example, say, "Is the gerbil big or small? Can you tell that to me so that I can write it down?" If a child does not offer anything (for example, an ELL child who is in the silent phase of learning English), do not force the issue. Encourage that child to illustrate the cover or help you with some other non-verbal activity.

Read all the ideas aloud. Add additional ideas as the children offer them.

Step Four: Read a book or show photographs of the topic. Add the ideas generated from the reading to your text. When the children have no more ideas, cut up the chart paper into strips, and write each child's idea in a complete sentence on a single strip. Glue each idea onto a piece of construction paper and help the children remember their ideas. Ask each child to draw a picture about his idea.

Step Five: As the children are drawing, make sure that they understand what their sentence says. Talk to them about making their pictures correspond to their words.

Step Six: Type up the children's sentences and glue them onto their pictures. Make a cover, and staple or bind the pages to make a book. Ask the children to illustrate the cover. Call them up one by one to draw a picture on the cover. Read the book aloud and then put it in the classroom library area. You also can send the book home with a different child each night to encourage literacy at home.

It is important to note that we are not exposing four-year-olds to writing process and writers' craft as a way to "push down" onto younger children a more sophisticated curriculum designed for older children. The process of making a book is an exciting activity for young children in its own right, and one in which the teacher does the actual writing and subsequent reading. The children are not expected to perform literacy skills for which they are not ready. They are not being asked to read the book on their own or to write prescribed sentences. They *are* being exposed to a system of *literary behavior* and sharing in the reward of seeing their book "published."

While we do not expect Head Start children to select the best words or sentence structures, we achieve a lot by exposing them to the concepts behind writing a book. They begin to understand that a book is a unified and organized collection of ideas written by people, that writing reflects speaking, that words and pictures work together to provide information, and that they can be authors who possess knowledge to share with others.

By modeling the process, young writers begin to see that some elements of emergent writer's craft fit in specific places of the writing process. For example, during the group pre-writing step, the young writers are learning how to brainstorm and choose a topic. As they gather their ideas and put them in some order, they are introduced to an understanding of grouping their ideas together in their rough draft. Later, as they begin to add to their ideas, they will be learning skills that they can apply during revising. While they learn how to listen for mistakes in grammar, usage, and conventions, they are receiving their first lessons in editing.

Making Class Books in Kindergarten

Goal: Introduce them to beginning craft elements and to the steps in the writing process.

For kindergartners, the process of making a class book is basically the same as for Head Start children, but each step is more developed. As she did with the Head Start lesson, the teacher does the writing but asks the children to make contributions that are more complex.

Step One: Have chart paper and markers ready to do a shared writing. Elicit ideas about a topic from the children, for example, dolphins. Tell the children that they are going to write a book about dolphins.

Step Two: Ask the children to tell what they know about dolphins. As each child shares an idea, write it down, followed by the child's name. As a group, read the ideas. Read a book about dolphins aloud and ask the children to listen for a new idea. Encourage the children to offer additional ideas they have learned from the book and write those down.

Step Three: Cut up the ideas and group them together as "chapter" headings that you create. Once you model chapter headings, children can begin to create the topics themselves. During shared writing, you can also begin to point out craft skills, such as active verbs, or convention skills, such as beginning a sentence with a capital letter and placing a period at the end of the sentence.

Step Four: Give each child a sentence and ask her to illustrate the idea in that sentence. As the children draw, make sure they know what their sentences say and that they are drawing pictures that reflect the content of the sentences.

Step Five: Assemble the book into chapters. In this step, the discussion to choose a topic qualifies as prewriting, and the first shared writing represents a rough draft where all ideas are gathered and recorded. The children are learning how to group ideas for their rough drafts when the ideas are first sorted and assembled. Encouraging them to add more information to the class book after you read a book to them on the same topic amounts to a first modeled lesson in the type of additive revision that is appropriate for first and second graders. Similarly, when you show them how to organize their class book contents into "chapters," you are modeling another organizational skill that roughly coincides with the revision step of writing process. As children check for whether they added periods and capitals, they are beginning to edit. After they add the illustrations, the book is assembled and "published."

At each stage, it is important for you to articulate each step of the writing process and model each craft skill. For example, before beginning the first shared writing, you might say, "As a pre-writing activity, let's gather all of our ideas so we can begin to write our rough draft."

Both the Head Start and the kindergarten lessons provide a lot of support from you. While you ask the children for ideas, you do the writing and determine when to move to the next stage. The children remain highly engaged and involved, however, and make their actual mark on the book when they begin to illustrate. By carefully considering the language levels and range of knowledge that all children bring from home, you honor your students and maintain a positive, collaborative climate in the classroom.

Making Class Books in First and Second Grade

Goal: Demonstrate the writing skills students will be expected to apply independently as they write a rough draft, revise, and edit their own pieces for practice and publication.

In first and second grades, the young writers make more of the choices, and the teacher provides less support. Depending on the class, a teacher can present the lesson in one piece or divide it over several days.

Step One: Gathering facts on a topic to begin a rough draft

Lead a shared writing, helping children gather their facts about the animal the class selected or about any other non-fiction topic. Label each idea with the name of the student who suggested it.

At this point, the children are collecting *facts* about the animal. If a student offers an opinion rather than a fact, take time to explain that an opinion is what we feel or believe and that others may feel differently. For example, if a student says, "Pandas are cute," validate his/her opinion, but gently suggest that someone else might think that they look scary. Help the student share a fact, rather than an opinion, such as, "Pandas have black circles around their eyes." The skill of discerning fact from opinion is an important critical thinking skill that children need to master to comprehend nonfiction.

Ask the children to read the ideas on the chart paper with you. Ask them if everyone gave an idea and add new ones that the children suggest.

Step Two: Adding more information to the rough draft

Have the shared writing completed in the last lesson ready, as well as additional chart paper for another shared writing.

Gather several non-fiction books on the same topic, and tell the children that you are going to read them a book about the same animal they selected. Ask them to listen carefully as you read because you want them to learn one or two more facts that they did not know. Explain that after you read, you will ask them to share the new ideas with the class and then add them to the class book.

After you read the book aloud, ask the children to tell you what they learned. Write down their ideas, followed by their names, on the chart paper. When a child offers an incomplete sentence or a sentence that is not grammatically correct, repeat his idea with the necessary adjustments, and then write it down accordingly. It is important that we both honor the child's *idea* and model correct language. If a student offers a fact that is already written, add her name next to the idea, too.

Ask the children to read the chart paper with you. Point out that by adding more information, they are making their book more interesting and useful for readers who wish to learn about the topic.

Step Three: Organizing the facts to begin revising

Gather library books that feature chapter headings, on any topic.

Have the shared writing from the previous lessons ready. Reread the shared writing and determine possible chapter categories. Usual groupings, where an animal is the topic, include physical characteristics, eating habits, behavior, and babies. Helping the children group their ideas together into "chapters" is the first step to teaching the skill of paragraphing.

First graders respond well to chapter headings such as "What Pandas Look Like," "What Pandas Eat," "Panda Behavior," and "Baby Pandas." (Second graders may be ready to decide on the appropriate chapter headings themselves during this shared time, based on their experiences with reading nonfiction library books). Type the chapter headings on a computer for the next step. Each heading should be on a separate sheet of paper.

Ask the children to read their facts with you as a shared reading. After reading, point out that some of the ideas belong together. For example, say, "I notice that many of you shared ideas about what pandas look like. Alex told us that they are black and white, Jennifer said that they have sharp teeth, and Jose told us that they have paws and sharp claws."

Then refer to the book you used as a read-aloud, and show the students how the author organized ideas together in chapters. Tell the students that they will do the same thing so that their readers will learn about what pandas look like, what they eat, etc. Tell them that as they organize their ideas, they are revising.

Lay the typed chapter headings on the rug. Cut up the shared writing into individual sentences and give each student his/her facts. Read the chapter headings to the children, and ask them to think about where each of their facts belongs. Ask each student to place his facts under the appropriate heading.

This task supports the children in a concrete way. As they see, touch, and manipulate the ideas, the relationships reveal themselves. They begin to understand the relationship between ideas and the concept that ideas, like objects, can be categorized. Offer as much help and support as necessary for this task, particularly through guided questioning. Say, for example, "The chapter called 'What Pandas Eat' will explain the food that pandas eat. Does your idea, that they eat bamboo, tell us about what they eat?" Modeling and practicing the sorting of facts into categories teaches the beginning concepts of building paragraphs.

After the children have placed their ideas under a chapter heading, read each group out loud. As you read each idea, allow the children to help decide whether that idea is in the correct group.

Together, count how many facts are under each chapter heading. Ask the students to name the chapters that only have one, two, or three facts. Ask them if they think readers will learn enough from only a couple of facts or if they should try to get more information to add. Show a chapter from a nonfiction book you have read to them, and examine the number of facts in one or two chapters.

Note: Most first-grade classes will provide only two or three facts in the beginning. If students already have more than three facts for each chapter the first time they try this, set the expected number higher for the next book.

If more information is needed, tell the students that you will go to the library and get books and magazines to read the following day. Tell them that you will read the books to them and that together you will "research" more information.

When you begin your shared research, remind them which chapters need more information, and read aloud from a book that provides that information. Then, do another shared writing.

Step Four: Checking the spelling of the high-frequency words to begin editing

Have the sentence strips ready, and provide a pencil for each child.

Tell the children that they are almost ready to publish their book but that they must first edit to check the spelling of the high-frequency words. Call the children's attention to the word wall. Have them read the words on the word wall with you. As you call out each word, ask the children to spell it aloud.

Ask the children to read their sentences and to find any high-frequency words on the word wall. Tell them that they will underline those words and check their spelling by comparing them to those on the word wall. As children work, walk around the room and make sure they are underlining the correct words.

Gather the children on the rug. For each of the words on the word wall, ask who found that word in their sentences. Ask volunteers to spell their words and confirm the correct spelling. Remind the children that this is called "editing" and that they should edit their writing every time they write a piece for publication. For additional editing, check for correct use of conventions, such as capital letters and ending punctuation.

Step Five: Illustrating and labeling

In this step, you will help children look at photographs and illustrations in nonfiction literature and evaluate how they work together with the words to enhance meaning. These photographs and illustrations become models that show the children how to add captions and labels to their own illustrations.

Print each child's sentence(s) on the computer. Use a large font so that the finished book can be used for a shared reading later. Glue each sentence onto the bottom of a half-sheet of construction paper. Give each child his or her page to illustrate.

Prepare chart paper and markers for shared writing. Gather books, pictures, and magazines with pictures of the animal about which the children have written. Have white drawing paper, pencils, and colored pencils or crayons ready.

Using nonfiction books, show the children photographs and illustrations of the animal. Talk about the visual features. For example, if the topic is the panda bear, ask the students questions, such as, "Does this picture of a panda look like a real panda?" Explain that nonfiction books teach facts, which are true, and that they use words *and* visual images to teach the readers.

Examine several nonfiction texts and do a shared writing to list the characteristics of photographs and true-to-life illustrations. Prompt ideas by asking questions such as, "What color is the panda?" "Are those the colors of a real panda?" "Do pandas have paws?" "Do you see paws in this picture?"

Help the children create a checklist on the chart paper that verifies that the colors are right, the parts of the panda's body are there, and the sizes are correct. Next, examine nonfiction labels in the read-aloud books you have already read. Point out that the labels are words that describe parts of the pictures.

Ask students to think about why authors might choose to include labels. Prompt answers that describe the importance of showing the reader parts of an animal that they might not know and of calling their attention to particular parts of the animal mentioned in the text. For example, say, "What if someone didn't know what a whisker is? Would the label next to the illustration help them learn?"

Do a modeled writing that describes a panda. For example, write, "Pandas have paws and sharp claws." Then ask the children what should be included in a drawing that would illustrate that fact. Demonstrate that they would need to draw a panda with paws and sharp claws, and label that part. Point out that drawings will help readers see what the writer means when he describes a panda.

Tell the children that they are going to practice illustrating and labeling. Remind them again that true-to-life nonfiction illustrations help teach the reader, just as the words do. Tell them that they may look at the photographs and illustrations in books, magazines, and pictures to help them think about the things that people can learn from them, and to draw an accurate picture of that idea. Give the children white drawing paper and pencils.

Note: The easiest labeling strategy for young children to implement is to draw a line from the picture to the word that labels it.

As you prepare the children to draw, show them the ideas they contributed to the class book to help them remember what they are to illustrate and label. Remind them to make sure their labels have been mentioned in their writing. For example, say, "If you wrote about a panda's fur, you should label the fur. That will help your readers know what fur is."

As children are drawing, walk around the room and talk to them about their drawings. If necessary, remind them to use the correct colors. After the children have finished the first drawings, give them the choice to redo their illustrations or to use their originals.

After the children are finished illustrating and labeling their final pictures, glue the illustrations onto the construction paper pages for the book.

Ask the children to bring their pages with them as they gather in a circle and hold up their pages. Ask them to look around at each other's work before laying the pages down in front of them.

Ask questions, based on the list of labeling categories that you and the class developed earlier. Some examples: "Who illustrated a page that shows what pandas eat?" "Who illustrated a page that shows what pandas look like?" "Who illustrated a page that shows where pandas live?"

Ask the children who added labels to explain them. Applaud for each other.

Step Six: Numbering the pages/creating a table of contents

Gather nonfiction books with tables of contents, pencils for children to use to number the book's pages, and chart paper and a marker to do a shared writing.

Explain to the children that they are going to number their pages and create a table of contents. Show examples of tables of contents. Tell them that, just like in books that you have read to them, their book needs a table of contents so that their readers know which page will tell them the information they need.

Hold up each chapter heading, glued onto a page, and collect all the pages that belong in that chapter. Then call up one student at a time to number a page. Using their chapter headings and their page numbers, do a shared writing to create a table of contents.

Step Seven: Type and print the table of contents and assemble the book

When the book is complete, arrange for the class to read it to other classes.

Refer to the students as "experts" on the animal chosen, and tell them that by reading the book to others, they are sharing information and helping others to learn about the animal. Add it to your class library area so that children can read it independently later.

Creating Books with Independent First and Second Graders

Goal: Independent practice

You can apply the same strategy of creating nonfiction class books to more sophisticated writers in first and second grade who are ready to try to create a book independently. These writers, who have previously participated in creating class books, now can write their own expository books. They have learned the steps of the process, have some understanding of how to address some early characteristics of writing, and are able to construct text independently. They are capable of reading well enough to research information from appropriately selected books and to revise their pieces by adding those new ideas.

Second grader Lanh, an ELL student who speaks Vietnamese at home, chose to write about polar bears. She began her rough draft by writing down the facts she already knew about polar bears. Then she consulted books and magazines to gather additional information, revising her rough draft by adding new facts. Lanh grouped similar ideas together by underlining the sentence categories in different colored crayons. For example, sentences that described what polar bears eat were underlined in orange, while sentences that told about their babies were underlined in purple. This was the basis for Lanh's chapters. She then edited her work and was ready to publish. A portion of Lanh's writing and her remarkable illustrations are shown below:

All About Polar Bears

Polar bears are white. They live in cold places. The light color of its fur matches the snow. This is called camouflage.

Polar bears eat fish. They eat lots of food to keep them warm.

Baby polar bears are called cubs. Mother polar bears teach her cubs how to catch fish.

We can see that Lanh's piece incorporates many good writing characteristics. She presents interesting ideas in an organized way, uses a variety of sentence structures and lengths, and chooses interesting words for which she provides explanations and definitions. Lanh's work clearly illustrates the benefits of the carefully scaffolded class book approach just described: she is capable of writing a well-organized and researched book all by herself.

Getting Topics from Books — Chart 4.1

Why Did I Choose This Book?	How Are the Events and Characters the Same as in Our Lives?
How Are the Events and Characters Different from Our Lives?	What Other Books Did the Book Remind Us of?

Writing-Goal Lessons

We are beginning to understand the value of sharing powerful lessons that model all aspects of writing. To make sure our instruction is meaningful and relevant, we must deliver the lesson to the right student at the right time. When we link the writing goals we have established for each child to an appropriate lesson, we can be sure that our instruction is meeting the specific writing needs of our students.

By knowing which writing goals students are working on, we can select the corresponding lessons and feel confident that they are meeting the students' instructional needs. We all know that even the most carefully planned lesson can be lost on a child who is not ready to learn the skills contained in the lesson. We must always base lessons on the needs of the students. When we identify and teach lessons according to writing goals, we fulfill our mission. The skills serve as a way to cluster children with similar learning needs and, when necessary, to provide one-on-one instruction.

This chapter offers a series of writing-goal lessons, organized according to the AEIOU system of the writing characteristic rubrics in Chapter 2. If a child's rubric analysis indicates, for example, a need for better skills in "E" – Expression of language, she receives an appropriate writing-goal lesson from that group.

The model lessons presented here represent a sampling, not an exhaustive list. They are presented within each category in order of difficulty, easiest first. Use them as they are or as models to develop your own specific lessons, always making sure that the lessons and expectations are appropriate for the child.

Developmental readiness is critically important when we analyze a child's writing sample and plan what to teach the child next. One child may be ready to learn a skill that the child next to him is not ready to grasp. When instruction is based on careful analysis of a child's present abilities and "next steps" to be taken, learning to write is a joyous experience for a child. She becomes aware that she is acquiring a powerful skill that allows her to join the ranks of writers in the literate society in which we all live.

Each of the lessons in this chapter, regardless of the genre it represents, corresponds to a specific writing goal. Some of the lessons focus on improving writer's craft. Others focus on helping the child understand the writing process or structural elements of specific genres. All help children attain good writing characteristics.

Characteristics of good writing remain consistent among all the different genres of writing. Whether a child is writing a recipe, a letter to her mother, a report on animals, or a letter to the president, the fundamental writing skills remain the same. <u>Children must write to an intended audience, maintain focus and organization, develop their ideas, express themselves clearly, and show mastery of English conventions.</u> The differences involve the tone and the structure of the writing (a letter needs a date and a greeting, a poem needs carefully chosen line breaks, a report needs a table of contents, a recipe needs a list of ingredients). While purposes such as "writing to inform" or "writing to persuade" determine the content, the fundamental purpose never changes: We write to communicate ideas.

Each lesson is taught in the context of what many teachers call "writer's workshop," an instructional framework developed by educators such as Donald Graves and Lucy Calkins. It is the classroom structure detailing the sequence of activities to be completed within a roughly 45-minute period. The more conducive our classroom atmosphere and structure is to writing, the more independent our students can be. The components of writer's workshop usually include:

- The lesson presented to children, either to the whole class or to a smaller group, depending on the children's goals.
- A time for quiet independent writing, when each child either begins a new rough draft or continues working on something started the

day before. These children will be revising or editing.

- Quiet individual "conferences" between the teacher and a child, designed to stimulate and encourage the child's work.
- A reflection of the day's work by the teacher and the whole class.

Within the writer's workshop, children work with the writing process—idea, rough draft, revision, editing, and publication. Of course, not all their pieces will be taken through all those stages.

Writing craft, on the other hand, comprises the specific skills that all writers use to attain the desired writing characteristics of the AEIOU rubrics. Teachers must model these skills for children to practice one at a time, generally using literature or a children's writing sample as the model. Marcia Freeman, the educator who has pioneered work with writing craft, calls the specific modeled skills, Target Skills.

Writing-Goal Lessons

Each lesson has six parts. The first four—**Teacher Preparation, Introduction, Addressing the Writing Goal,** and **Final Preparation**— prepare children to write. During the next part of the lesson, **Individual Conferences,** you confer as the children work on their pieces. It is important for you to walk around the room, reminding children to work quietly, and whispering words of praise and encouragement. This is also a good opportunity to assess the writing behavior of the children, using the Observation Sheet shown in Chapter Two, Chart 1.1 on page 18. As you confer with a child, you can refer to the previous lesson if the child's current writing indicates a need for further instruction.

As each lesson explains, children only write once they have indicated that they have their ideas ready. While they may need to confer with their teacher once they reach a certain point in their writing, random discussions between children should be discouraged. A child who asks a question to a neighbor might be interrupting the other child's thoughts, which unfairly disrupts the work of another young writer.

The last part of each lesson, **Final Reflections,** offers children the opportunity to share their work and allows you to assess each child's writing quickly. I tend to stay away from the common practice of allowing every child to read his writing aloud because the result is often long and tedious. Instead, I suggest that the children sit in a circle and hold up their writing so that their classmates can see their work. Quickly, you will be able to get a sense of what each child did that day, and the children enjoy seeing all the other papers.

Finally, ask children to raise their hands if they performed a particular writing strategy, indirectly reminding them of the strategies they should be using. For example, by asking, "Who remembered to use the word 'wall'?" children are able to receive validation for using that strategy, or they are reminded to do so the next time they write.

How Writing-Goal Lessons Support ELL Children

Writer's workshop in a classroom of ELL children has a different tone, a different rhythm, and a different pace.

Some of the specific characteristics of the ELL writer's workshop are

- They need more time to prepare to write, by having ample opportunity to express their ideas orally.

- The Final Preparation section in each lesson holds additional significance for ELL children. While all young children benefit from hearing their ideas and receiving validation from their teacher, the ELL child also uses this occasion as an opportunity to practice the English language in a supportive environment.

- Conferencing with the teacher plays a triple role: it helps with revisions, it increases English vocabulary, *and* it builds English syntax.

All children find that the task of revision helps them improve word selection, sentence structures, and organization. Revision additionally gives ELL children an excellent opportunity to help English vocabulary development. If, for example, a child has written the word "good" numerous times, his teacher can offer him other words for "good," such as "wonderful," "great," or "terrific."

Children who are learning English often apply the language structure from their first language towards their attempts in English. For example, the Spanish adjective is written after the noun it modifies, unlike English, so that Spanish-speaking children may well first write the noun and then the adjective. As we help ELL children edit, we allow them to hear the correct structure of English. We can say, for example, "In books, we say it like this" or "When we speak English, we say it like this."

One of the most effective ways to create an environment that honors the needs of ELL children was developed by Joanne Busalacchi, a principal in a school where I once taught. In this model, an ELL teacher who is also skilled in teaching reading and writing teaches a whole ELL class for half the day, taking full responsibility for the language arts instruction. By focusing on their English language development through speaking, listening, reading, and writing, the teacher provides her students with a strong foundation of language in a safe, nurturing, and supportive environment. She is able to maintain the tone, the rhythm, and the pace geared towards children learning English, while skillfully teaching the craft of writing. Then, for the second half of each day, the children join their "homeroom" classes, where they hear English modeled by their English-speaking peers and where they can use their developing English as they participate in math, science, and social studies lessons.

The writing sample below shows the remarkable achievement of an ELL child who learned using the half-day model. The writing sample represents a second-grade ELL child's response to the third prompt of the year, asking him to tell about a special day at school.

Young Author's Conference

Young Authors Conference.
When it's was Young Author's Conference
Day, I went where I needed to go, so I can read my
book. I was the last to read the book in the group.
I was very bored because the kids took along
time to read their book. And when it's was
to read the book
my turn, a women talked in the microphone.
She said "If your group is done eat the
cookies and the juice." When she said
that I was embassed from insid
my self. When it's was time to go
Mrs. Emmer saw my book. she said
it's was great. I felt happy when
she said that. I like Young Authors
Conference Day.

When we simply take Title I ELL children out of their classrooms and try to teach them the English words for fruits, vegetables, colors, and animals, and drill them on their letters and numbers, we deprive them of the opportunity to learn the academic concepts and the language that their English-speaking peers learn at home. They move from kindergarten to first grade and from first grade to second grade. With low test scores, they are labeled as "at-risk," and as their teachers maintain low expectations of them, they fall further and further behind.

On the other hand, when ELL children are given rich and in-depth writing instruction in a self-contained classroom taught by a teacher who is knowledgeable in English-language acquisition, they flourish.

Writing-Goal Lessons

Lessons on "A" - Addressing Your Audience
Lesson 1: Asking the Reader a Question
<u>Rubric Category:</u> Addressing your Audience
<u>Writing Goal:</u> Using questions to engage your reader

Teacher Preparation

Brave Irene by William Steig; *Today I Feel Silly* by Jamie Lee Curtis; and *So You Want to Be President?* by Judith St. George and David Small.

Introduction

Read each book once for the children to enjoy. Then read each book again and ask the children to listen for the questions the author asks. The questions are, "Would you like to hear the rest?" in *Brave Irene*; "How do you feel today?" in *Today I Feel Silly*; and "Do you have pesky brothers and sisters?" in *So You Want to Be President*?

Addressing the Writing Goal

After reading the books a second time, ask the children to point out where the authors ask the questions. Then, write the questions on chart paper. Ask the children to explain why the authors ask these questions and to whom they are directing the question. Discuss the technique of asking questions, and explain that authors do this to "talk to" their readers and make them pay attention as they read.

Final Preparation

Tell the children that as they write, they should choose a place to ask their readers a question.

Individual Conferences

As the children are writing, observe if they are incorporating the technique of asking their readers a question. If they are not, ask them to think of a question to write in a place of their choosing.

Final Reflection

Gather the children on the rug, and ask them to raise their hand if they asked their readers a question. Allow children to share their questions. Ask them if they think the question helped their readers focus better on the writing.

Lesson 2: Writing a Persuasive Letter

Rubric Category: Addressing your Audience

Writing Goal: Explaining actions, feelings, and events to intended audience using a unique, expressive voice

Teacher Preparation

Two nonfiction books about the same animal.

Introduction

Tell students that you are trying to decide about which animal they should learn. Tell them that they will be making a class big book about an animal and they need to choose which one. For example, show them a book about an elephant and a book about a dog.

Addressing the Writing Goal

Explain that you would like them first to tell you the animal they choose and then persuade you why their choice is a good one. Emphasize that they must state their choice in a complete sentence. For example, they should say, "I want to make a book about an elephant" or "I want to make a book about dogs." You might want to go around the circle and allow each student to state his choice before using any persuasive ideas. Then ask each student to give you two reasons why you should select the animal they chose. Encourage them to explain their feelings with words that will help you understand their reason. Give them examples, such as, "I just love dogs and want to learn as much as I can about them!" Students might say, "I have a dog and I love dogs" or "I saw an elephant at the zoo" or "I want to learn about elephants." All ideas should be accepted.

Note: Use the term "persuade" as often as possible so that the children learn its meaning. They may need many opportunities to practice persuasive speaking. Class discussions should occur for several days before writing begins. As we have discussed before, young children greatly benefit from talking about their ideas before writing. They need to hear their ideas so that they can formulate their thoughts. They also need to understand the concept of "audience" and are able to learn that concept by practicing to an audience of teachers and peers. As they begin to learn about persuasive writing, they must first understand how to persuade an audience **orally**.

Final Preparation

Model the format of a friendly letter. Include the date, the salutation, body of the letter, the closing, and the signature. Allow students to share in the writing by calling each one up to the chart paper to show where the parts of a friendly letter belong on the page. Then remind students about the two animals you suggested to them during the introduction. Tell them that you would like them to write a letter to you persuading you to choose the animal they like best. Remind them that the first sentence in the body of the letter should tell you which animal they prefer. Give them an opportunity to share their first sentence aloud to make sure they are ready to write. Leave the model on chart paper for them to refer to as they write.

Individual Conferences

While students are writing, quietly confer with individual children about their format and persuasive argument. Point out the model of a friendly letter if they need to refer to it. If they do not include more than one persuasive idea, talk to them and ask them questions to help them generate more ideas. For example, ask, "Do you think that animal would be interesting? Why don't you write, 'I think it would be interesting to learn about elephants.'?"

Final Reflection

Gather students on the rug in a circle. Ask them to hold up their letters so that their classmates can see them. Ask students to raise their hands if they:

- Wrote the date.
- Wrote a salutation.
- Remembered how to persuade you to choose their animal and included their ideas in the body of the letter.
- Wrote a closing.
- Signed their names.

Applaud for each other. Tell them that you will read their letters and decide which book to read (Read *both* books to validate the efforts of all the children!).

Lesson 3: Writing a Persuasive Letter

<u>Rubric Category:</u> Addressing your Audience

<u>Writing Goal:</u> Explaining actions, feelings, and events to audience, using a unique voice

Introduction

Remind students about the story *The Three Bears*. Ask them to share what happened when Goldilocks entered the home of the three bears. Ask if they think she should have gone in. Tell them that they will be writing a letter to Goldilocks to persuade her either not to do that again or to go back to the home of the three bears and have another adventure.

Addressing the Writing Goal

Allow students time to think about what they would like to write to Goldilocks. Ask for a show of hands of those who think she should return to the house and then of those who think she should not. Encourage students to express their ideas aloud. Tell them first to state what they will tell Goldilocks to do and then to explain their reasons.

Final Preparation

Ask students to state the parts of a friendly letter and remind them to include all parts as they write (The parts are date, opening, body of letter, closing, and signature).

Individual Conferences

While students are writing, quietly confer with individuals to make sure they remember their persuasive arguments and include them in the letter. If they are not following the format of a letter, show them a model on chart paper and guide them through the steps.

Final Reflection

Gather on the rug in a circle. Ask the children to hold up their letters so that their classmates can see their work. Ask students to raise their hands if they:

- Wrote the date.
- Wrote an opening greeting.
- Remembered how to persuade Goldilocks to return to the house or not.
- Wrote a closing.
- Signed their names.

Applaud for each other.

Lesson 4: Using Words to Describe Things (Adjectives)

<u>Rubric Category:</u> Expression of Language

<u>Writing Goal:</u> Using interesting words

Teacher Preparation

A House for Hermit Crab by Eric Carle, chart paper, and markers.

Introduction

Read the book once for the children to enjoy. Read it again a second or third time, and ask the children to listen for words that describe things. Remind them that these words are called "adjectives."

Addressing the Writing Goal

Then ask the children to list all the describing words that they heard. You may need to read the book one more time, asking the children to give a hand signal each time they hear one. Record the words on the chart paper. Examples are "snug," "strong," "plain," "beautiful," "small," "little," "hard," "pretty," "crusty," "neat," "tidy," "sharp," "prickly," "fierce," "spiky," "dark," "dim," "gloomy," "murky," "bright," "smooth," "sturdy," and "perfect."

Final Preparation

Tell the children that they can use describing words when they write, to make their writing more interesting for their readers. Ask them to close their eyes and picture a monster or an animal. Then ask them to each think of a sentence that describes the creature, and then say their sentence in preparation for writing. Make sure their sentence contains adjectives.

Individual Conferences

If a child is struggling, encourage him to draw a picture that shows exactly what his creature looks like. Then talk to him about what you see, emphasizing adjectives in your description. Ask him to write a description of his creature.

Final Reflection

Gather the children on the rug, and ask them if they would like to share their work. As children read their descriptions, list the adjectives on chart paper. Display the list in the room, and tell them that you would like them to use some adjectives each time they write.

Lesson 5: Writing a Simile

Rubric Category: Expression of Language

Writing Goal: Choosing words that place pictures in the reader's mind

Teacher Preparation

Quick as a Cricket by Audrey Wood, chart paper, and markers.

Introduction

Read the book once as a read-aloud so that the children can enjoy the story. Read the book a second time, asking the children to listen to the pattern of the sentences.

Addressing the Writing Goal

Write a few sentences from the book on chart paper. Use two colors: one for the words "I am as … as a…," and one for the adjective and the noun. For example, "I am as *mean* as a *shark.*" Ask the children to create their own similes about themselves, using the same kind of sentence. Encourage them to state their sentence aloud so that you can write it on the chart paper. If a child is having difficulty thinking of a simile, prompt her by asking questions. Ask, for example, "Are you nice?" "What animal is also nice?" "Are you as nice as that animal?" After everyone has contributed an idea, use the sentences to conduct a shared reading.

Final Preparation

Cut the chart paper into individual sentence strips, and give each child her sentence. Make sure each child is able to read (or remember) the sentence. Ask the children to take the sentences to their seats, and ask them to illustrate the idea.

Individual Conferences

Walk around and make sure all the children are working. If a child is having difficulty beginning, ask him to read his sentence with you. Then ask him what he should put in his picture.

Final Reflection

Gather the children on the rug, and ask them to hold up their pictures. Then ask them to read their ideas. Display the pictures and sentences on the wall, and tell the children that you would like them to use some of the sentences in their writing.

Lesson 6: Writing Synonyms
__Rubric Category:__ Expression of Language
__Writing Goal:__ Using interesting words

Teacher Preparation

A book that emphasizes adjectives to read aloud, such as *Big* by Keith Haring, is a good choice for ELL and for preK and kindergarten children.

Introduction

Read the book that you have chosen as a read-aloud and a second time for the children to listen for the descriptive words. Tell them that sometimes authors use different words that have the same meaning and that these words are called "synonyms." Explain that authors use synonyms rather than using the same words over and over, which makes their writing more enjoyable to read and to listen to.

Addressing the Writing Goal

After the second or third reading, ask the children to list some of the describing words and write them on chart paper. After writing each word and discussing their similar meanings, choose another word such as "good." Ask the children to list other words that also mean "good." Write the words on chart paper.

Final Preparation

Write the word "little" on chart paper. Ask the children to go to their seats and write as many synonyms for the word as they can.

Individual Conferences

If a child cannot think of any synonyms, prompt her by giving her a sentence with the word "little." Then ask her to repeat the sentence and to substitute the word "little" with another word that means the same thing.

Final Reflection

Gather the children on the rug and ask them to raise their hand if they would like to offer a synonym for "little." List the words on chart paper, and then display the list on the wall. Tell the children that you would like them to use some of the words the next time they write.

Lesson 7: Describing a Character
Rubric Category: Expression of Language
Writing Goal: Using adjectives to create sensory images

Teacher Preparation

Prepare a list of items that will be easy for children to describe. For example, a rainbow is something that children can say is colorful or pretty. An elephant, which children may say is big and gray, is another example. Have the list written on chart paper so that the class will be able to see it, and have all materials ready for writer's workshop.

Introduction

Tell students that good writers use descriptive words when they write. Explain that one type of word that helps make writing more interesting is a word that tells how something looks. Remind them of the previous lessons on adjectives. Encourage them to use specific words as they describe.

Addressing the Writing Goal

Show the children pictures of people and animals. Ask them to describe the appearance of them. Write their descriptions on chart paper, and make suggestions of more "wonderful words." Remind them that the words they choose can paint a picture in the reader's mind. For example, if a child writes, "The girl is pretty," help him reconstruct his sentence to be more specific and descriptive, such as "The girl's eyes were as brown as chocolate milk."

Final Preparation

Tell the children that you would like them to describe a character that they create. Explain that they should describe what their character looks like, using wonderful describing words.

Offer some examples, such as, "There was once a small, furry dog. He was brown with white spots and he had a long tail." "A little girl had long black hair, sparkling green eyes, and a bright yellow dress." Allow students time to think about their character. Ask them to share their descriptions aloud as rehearsal for writing. As they get ready to write at their seats, suggest that they first draw a picture and then write a description.

Individual Conferences

If a student spends more than 5-10 minutes on his picture, encourage him to begin to write. Conduct quiet conferences, reminding students to use specific words that paint a picture in words for the reader.

Final Reflection

Ask students to gather on the rug, sit in a circle, and hold up their work. Allow them to look around at each other's pictures and writing. Ask students to raise their hand if they:

- Used words that described the size of their character.
- Used words that described the color of their character.
- Used wonderful words.

Lesson 8: Describing an Action (Verbs)

Rubric Category: **Expression of Language**

Writing Goal: **Using a strong verb**

Teacher Preparation

A House For Hermit Crab by Eric Carle and *The Napping House* by Audrey Wood.

Introduction

Read each book once for all the children to enjoy. Read the books a second or third time, telling the children to listen to all the ways the author describes what each character does.

Addressing the Writing Goal

Ask the children to list the words they hear that describe what characters do. Examples are " wiggling," "waggling," "swayed," "signaled," "creaked," "crawling," "grazed," "wandered," and "murmured" from *A House For Hermit Crab* and "bites," "scares," "claws," "thumps," "bumps," and "breaks" from *The Napping House.*

Final Preparation

Call out some of the words and ask the children to act them out. Then, ask them to draw a picture of themselves performing one of those actions, or any other action, and to write the sentence that tells about it. For example, hey could write, "I bite my hamburger" or "I wiggle in my bed."

Individual Conferences

As the children draw their pictures, quietly ask them to tell you what action they are showing. If a child is unable to think of the action word, ask her a question, such as, "Are you jumping?" Then help her formulate her sentence.

Final Reflection

Gather the children on the rug, and ask them to hold up their pictures. Offer to read their sentences aloud, and list any new action words to the previous list. Display the words in the room, on a poster, or in a book that the children can reference as they write, and tell them that you would like them to use action words the next time they write.

Lesson 9: Using Adverbs to Describe Actions

Rubric Category: Expression of Language

Writing Goal: Beginning sentences in different ways

Teacher Preparation

Dr. DeSoto by William Steig and *Fish Is Fish* by Leo Lionni, chart paper, and markers.

Introduction

Read each book once for the children to enjoy. Then read each book a second or third time, and ask them to pay attention to the words that tell **how** the characters do things.

Addressing the Writing Goal

Ask the children to list the words they hear that describe how the characters do things. Examples include, "bitterly," "bravely," and "promptly" from *Dr. DeSoto* and "triumphantly," "excitedly," "mysteriously," "impatiently," and "gently" from *Fish Is Fish*. Write the words on chart paper as the children identify them. Select some of the words for the children to act out so that they can see the meaning of the words and understand their power for imagery. Again, tell the children that the words describe **how** characters do things and that the words make the writing more interesting to read.

Final Preparation

Ask the children to imagine that they are doing something they enjoy. Give suggestions, such as playing, doing a sport, drawing, or eating. Then ask them to imagine **how** they are doing these things. Suggest adverbs, such as happily, quietly, beautifully, quickly, and so on. Explain that they can use these kinds of words, called "adverbs," when they write. Tell them that one way to use them is to begin a sentence with an adverb. Show some examples, such as, "Happily, I went home" and "Suddenly, we heard a noise" and "Quietly, the children sat down." Ask them to try to begin as least one sentence with an adverb each time they write.

Individual Conferences

Walk around the room and quietly ask individual children to show you where they have begun a sentence with an adverb. If they are struggling, choose one of their sentences that talks about an action and suggest putting an adverb at the beginning.

Final Reflection

Gather on the rug and ask the children to hold up their work. Ask the children to read their writing or offer to read it for them. Ask the children to identify the sentences that they began with an adverb.

Lesson 10: Using Other Words for "Said"

Rubric Category: Expression of Language

Writing Goal: Using more specific words to describe actions

Teacher Preparation

The Very Busy Spider by Eric Carle and *Dr. DeSoto* by William Steig, chart paper, and markers.

Introduction

Read each book once for the children to enjoy. Read the books a second or third time, reminding the children to listen to all the ways the author describes the ways the characters talk.

Addressing the Writing Goal

Ask the children to list the words they hear that describe how characters talk. Examples from *The Very Busy Spider* are "bleated," "grunted," "barked," "called," "crowed," and "asked" and "shouted," "wept," "whispered," "gasped," "announced," and "yelled" from *Dr. DeSoto.*

Final Preparation

Tell the children that they can use these words in their own writing. Explain that the words can describe the way a person sounds when he is talking. For example, if a person is angry, they can use the word "barked" or "snapped" or "shouted." Ask them to draw a picture of themselves talking to someone and to think of what they might be saying. Instruct them to draw first and then to write. For example, they could draw themselves walking in their house and write, "'I'm home,' I announced."

Individual Conferences

Ask the questions, "Do you talk to someone?" "What do you say?" "How do you feel when you are talking?" Refer the children to the list on the chart paper to help them select an appropriate word for "said."

Final Reflection

Gather the children on the rug, and ask them to hold up their work. Ask permission to read their sentences. Talk about all the different ways they chose to write, "said." Tell them that you will look for some of these words in their future writing.

Lesson 11: Saying "I like" in Different Ways
Rubric Category: Expression of Language
Writing Goal: Beginning sentences in different ways

Teacher Preparation

Mentally prepare several sentences beginning with "I like" to write in front of the class. Chart paper, markers, and all materials for the children to do their own writing.

Introduction

Write a modeled writing in front of the class about things you like. Begin every sentence with "I like." When you have finished writing, ask the students to read your writing with you. As you read, emphasize the words "I like." For example, "**I like** to read books." "**I like** books about famous people." "**I like** to learn about their lives." "**I like** to write." "**I like** to write letters to my friends."

Addressing the Writing Goal

Primary children can learn to substitute a summary sentence for "I like," using phrases such as "I am interested in" or "I have fun …" or "My favorite…" "I enjoy…" Model the choices, and allow the children to practice using these phrases in their pieces.

Ask the students what they think about your sentences. Ask them if they think your writing would be better if you did not begin every sentence the same way. Tell the children that you would like them to help you make your writing better. Explain that you want to change your sentences so that they all do not begin with "I like." Make a chart with two columns, and write, "I like" several times down the left column. For each time you write "I like," show the children other ways to explain that you like something.

Final Preparation

Remind the children that when they are writing about something they like, they should also try to write, "I like" in different ways. Ask them to give you some suggestions of other ways to say, "I like," and then encourage them to use those phrases in their writing.

Individual Conferences

While walking around the room and maintaining a quiet environment, check that all children are writing. If a child is writing, "I like," quietly confer with him about other expressions to use.

Final Reflection

Gather the children in a circle, and ask them to hold up their work for everyone to see. Ask the children to raise their hand if they:

- Wrote about things they like.
- Thought of another way to say, "I like."

Lessons on "I" - Ideas

Lesson 12: Getting Ideas from Other People's Stories
<u>Rubric Category:</u> **Ideas**

<u>Writing Goal:</u> **Selecting a topic**

<u>Emergent Writing Goals:</u> **Drawing a picture, writing a word, writing a phrase, writing a sentence**

Teacher Preparation
Chart paper and markers. Think about an event in your life that you can share with the children. (Children are very interested in hearing about their teachers' lives!)

Introduction

Gather on the rug, and tell the children you have a story to share with them. After you have finished sharing your story, make the following request: "Now tell me about something that has happened to you. It can be similar to mine or something different."

The purpose of this request is to help children find topics for writing. It does not matter if they share something unrelated or something very much the same. Whatever a child offers should be met with interest and enthusiasm so that they feel that they have something to share. Try to make a connection between your idea and each child's idea. For example, if your anecdote related to a birthday party and a child chose to tell about Christmas, you could say, "Did you all notice that Maria told us about her Christmas presents after hearing about my birthday presents? Maria did what all good writers do. She listened to my ideas, and then she thought about an idea from her own life. Maria, you're thinking like a writer!"

Addressing the Writing Goal

Explain that each of the children's ideas would be a good topic about which to draw and write. Emphasize the point that all good writers listen to ideas around them and then find an idea to write about.

Final Preparation

Ask the children if they are ready to write. Ask them to tell you what topic they have chosen and if they have lots to tell about that topic. Explain that choosing a good topic is the first thing that all good writers do and that they are showing you that they are already good writers.

Individual Conferences

Encourage children to both draw and write. Use their pictures to stimulate more writing. For example, you might say, "Your picture really shows how happy you were. I see a big smile on your face! If you write about how happy you felt, your readers would know more about that special day in your life."

Final Reflection

Gather on the rug in a circle, and ask the children to hold up their work. Allow them a minute to look at each other's writing. Then ask the following questions:

- Who chose a topic about something that happened to them?

- Who chose a happy topic?
- Who chose a sad topic?
- Who drew a picture about their topic?
- Who wrote words about their topic?

Lesson 13: Adding Details

Rubric Category: Ideas

Writing Goal: Creates Supporting Sentences to Develop Ideas

Teacher Preparation

Prepare a topic to write on chart paper in front of the children. Materials for writing (writing notebooks, pencils, crayons).

Introduction

Tell the children the topic you have selected and explain why you chose that topic. For example, say, "Today I am going to write a rough draft about my brother's wedding. I have been thinking about his wedding a lot because it was such a special day, so I know it is a good topic for me." Demonstrate your modeled writing, thinking aloud about why you are including particular details. For example, "I think I'll write about the cake. It was so pretty and so delicious! I know my readers will enjoy reading about it." Include no more than three sentences.

Addressing the Writing Goal

Finish writing and read your sentences aloud. Ask the children if there is anything else they would like to know about the wedding. As each question is asked, acknowledge that your writing would be better if you included that information, and add the sentence that answers the question. For example, if a child asks, "Did you dance?" you might say, "Yes! I danced a lot! I'm sure my readers would like to hear about that. I'm going to tell about the dancing." Then add a sentence about dancing at the wedding. Explain that describing an experience by thinking about what readers would like to hear makes writing more enjoyable to read. Tell the children that we call this part of the writing process "revising."

Final Preparation

Ask the children to choose a rough draft from a previous day and to think about adding one or two sentences to make the writing more interesting. Tell them again that this is called "revising." Ask if anybody would like to read their rough draft aloud and then to tell what they are going to add.

Individual Conferences

Walk around the room, maintaining a quiet working environment. Offer praise and encouragement, using a quiet whisper. If a child needs help, ask a question about the picture or the writing, and suggest that he/she write more to answer your question.

Final Reflection

Gather the children on the rug in a circle, and ask them to hold up their work so that their peers can see it. Ask children to raise their hands if they:

- Read their rough draft.
- Added more ideas.
- Used the word wall.
- Used sound spelling.

Tell them that good writers do all these things. Applaud for each other

Note: It is important to include the same questions about the word wall and sound spelling that were asked after the previous lesson on writing a rough draft. Children need a lot of practice with these skills.

Lesson 14: Using Symbols to Add Details
Rubric Category: Ideas
Writing Goal: Understanding how to insert new information

Teacher Preparation

Choose a confident student who has a rough draft that needs to be revised. Ask her permission to show her writing to the class so that everyone can help her revise it. Remind her of when the class helped you revise your writing. Make an overhead transparency of the child's writing to show on an overhead projector.

Introduction

Tell the class that the student has agreed to share her writing with them so that they can help her revise her rough draft. Show the student's writing on the overhead projector and read it aloud.

Addressing the Writing Goal

Ask the class if anyone has a question to ask the writer. Remind them that asking a writer questions helps her see that her audience is interested in what she has written and wants to know more. Explain that the questions will help her revise her writing to make it more interesting to read. When a child asks a question, allow the writer to answer. Then ask her, "Do you think your writing would be more interesting if you added that information?" If the writer says yes, allow her to add the new information onto the transparency so that all the children can see it. Repeat this process once or twice more. When the writer has finished writing, read the work aloud. Praise her for sharing her work and for working hard on revising.

Note: If there is no space for the writer to add another sentence, show her how to make a little star or caret in the spot where the sentence needs to go, and then write the idea somewhere else on the paper. Explain that she can insert the sentence in the correct spot later.

Final Preparation

Explain to the class that describing feelings and events as if you were talking makes the writing more enjoyable to read. Remind them that we call this part of the writing process **revising.** Ask the children to choose a rough draft from another day, and to add one or two sentences. Before the children go to their seats, make sure they each have chosen parts of their writing that they will revise. Suggest that they insert a symbol like a star or caret to indicate the places where they will revise.

Individual Conference

While maintaining a quiet working environment, walk around the room and make sure that each child is engaged in writing. If a child seems to need help, ask a question about his picture or his writing, and suggest that he write more to answer your question.

Final Reflection

Gather the children in a circle and ask them to hold up their work. Ask them to raise a hand if they did each of the following:

- Read their rough draft.
- Decided where to add more details.
- Used sound spelling and the word wall.

Lesson 15: Creating a Web AFTER Writing a Rough Draft

Rubric Category: Ideas

Writing Goal: Finding a meaningful topic; developing ideas

Note: Present this lesson <u>numerous times</u> before you ask the children to create their own webs. This is a more advanced lesson.

Teacher Preparation

Mentally prepare a few sentences that tell about an experience you have had. Make sure that each sentence describes a different aspect of the experience. For example, "My daughter had a birthday on Monday. She turned seven years old. She got lots of presents. We also had cake." Have chart paper and markers ready, as well as all materials necessary for children to do their own writing.

Introduction

Tell the children that you are going to do a modeled writing for them. Explain that a modeled writing means that you are going to do the thinking and the writing and that they are going to listen and watch. Tell them that after you have finished, you are going to read your sentences and decide if you have written enough.

Addressing the Writing Goal

Before you write, tell the children why you have chosen your idea. In my example, I might say, "I am going to write about my daughter's birthday because it just passed and I remember a lot about the day." As you write, think aloud about why you are selecting the ideas that you are writing. For example, say, "I think I'll tell about the cake." When you have finished writing, say, "I want to think about each of my sentences to help me decide if I have written enough information."

Tell the children that one way to figure this out is to make a web that shows all the information you have in your writing. Show the children what you mean by a "web" by drawing a circle, a few lines radiating from the circle, and smaller circles at the end of each line. In the central web, write the main topic of your writing. In my example, this would be, "My daughter's birthday." Tell the children that you are writing the main idea of your topic in the middle circle because everything in your writing talks about that idea.

Read your sentences aloud, one at a time, explaining the category in which each belongs. Then, in one of the outer circles, write a name for that category.

In my example, the first sentence tells about **when** the birthday occurred. Thus, I would write, "when" in one of the circle. My second sentence tells about my daughter's **age**, so in one of the circles I would write, "Her age."

Do the same for each sentence. When you have finished categorizing the sentences, ask the children to help you count how many different kinds of ideas you have. In my example, there are four sentences about four different aspects of my main idea.

Note: As children begin to produce more writing, use a web to show how many categories of ideas you have **and** to show the number of ideas you have within each category. In the above example, I might describe the way the cake looked and tasted and then count the number of ideas I shared about the cake. In the circle that says "the cake," I would then write a number that shows the number of my ideas about the cake. In this way, children are encouraged to add more and more details, and they are given a graphic reminder of how many details they have provided.

Final Preparation

Tell the children that you would like them to choose an idea about which to write. Remind them that the best ideas are the ones about which we know and care a lot. Explain that you would like them to write about one main idea and to write three or four sentences that tell about different parts of their idea. Before the children go off to write, ask them to tell you their idea.

Individual Conferences

As the children are writing, walk around the room and maintain a quiet work environment. Make sure that the children are beginning to work. If a child seems to be having difficulty getting started, suggest that he begin by drawing a picture. You can also remind him of the idea he shared before going to his seat. As you look at the children's writing, select a child who has written three or four sentences that fit the criteria of the assignment. Ask her if you may use her writing to create a web and show it to the class.

Final Reflection

Gather the children on the rug. Create a web of the child's writing that you selected. Ask the child the following questions:

- How did you choose your idea?
- How did you know that it would be a good idea for you?
- What is your main idea?
- About how many different parts of your idea did you write?

Lessons on "O" - Organization

Lesson 16: Writing an Opening Sentence that "Hooks" the Reader

Rubric Category: Word Choice and Organization

Writing Goal: Beginning a piece with an exclamation or a rich description

Teacher Preparation

Gather the books *At the Crossroads* by Rachel Isadora and *The Emperor's Egg* by Martin Jenkins.

Introduction

Read each book aloud for enjoyment. As you read each book a second time, ask the children to pay close attention to the first sentence.

Addressing the Writing Goal

Write the opening sentence from each book on chart paper. First, ask the children what they notice about each sentence. Then, point out that each sentence "hooks" the reader and makes them want to read more. Explain that the beginning sentence in *At the Crossroads*, "Today our fathers are coming home!" shows that the children in the book are excited. Explain that the exclamation point helps the reader share the writer's excitement and want to keep reading. Next, refer to the nonfiction selection, *The Emperor's Egg*, which begins, "Down at the very bottom of the world, there's a huge island that's almost completely covered in snow and ice." Pont out that the story begins with a wonderful description that puts a picture in our minds and makes us curious to read more.

Final Preparation

Give the children time to think of a topic for writing. Then, ask them to think of an opening sentence that introduces their topics in an interesting way. Their topics can be fiction or nonfiction. Ask them to tell you their first sentence, and then send them to begin to write.

Individual Conferences

As children are writing, make sure they include an opening sentence.

Final Reflection

Gather the children on the rug, and ask if anyone would like to share his writing. Offer to read his writing aloud so that you can model expressive reading. Tell the children that you would like them to remember to write an opening sentence each time they write, using an exclamation or a wonderful description.

Lesson 17: *Writing a Powerful Ending Sentence*

<u>Rubric Category</u>: Organization

<u>Writing Goal</u>: Writing a strong ending that describes a feeling, a wish, or a hope.

Teacher Preparation

Gather a group of books that share a similar ending structure. For example, gather the books *Alexander and the Wind-Up Mouse* by Leo Lionni, *Yoko* by Rosemary Wells, *Where the Wild Things Are* by Maurice Sendak, *Koala Lou* by Mem Fox, and *When Sophie Gets Angry-Really, Really Angry…* by Molly Bang. Each of these books ends with a short sentence beginning with the word, "And," and leaves the reader with a warm, happy feeling.

Introduction

Read each book over the course of a few days. Read each book once for the children to enjoy and a second time for the children to attend to the ending sentence.

Addressing the Writing Goal

Write each of the ending sentences on chart paper. They are, in order of the books mentioned above: *"And there they danced until dawn," "And they couldn't have asked for anything more," "And it was still hot," "And she hugged her for a very long time,"* and *"And Sophie isn't angry anymore."* Ask the children what they notice about each of the sentences. Discuss the way in which each sentence describes a feeling. Explain that one way a writer can end a piece is to describe a feeling.

Final Preparation

Discuss the technique of ending with a sentence that shares a feeling, a hope, or a wish. Ask the children to think of a short story, of just a few sentences, where two characters have a problem, solve the problem, and feel happy at the end, or to write about something that happened in their own lives. Encourage them to end their writing piece with a feeling, a wish, or a hope. Model this with examples, such as "I hope I go back again soon" or "I wish that had never happened." Make sure the children have an idea for writing before they go back to their seats to write.

Individual Conferences

As children are writing, encourage them either to write a piece that includes a problem and a solution or to write about their own lives. They should try to end their pieces with a feeling, a wish, or a hope.

Final Reflection

Gather the children on the rug, and ask if anyone would like to read her story. Offer to read the story for the child, and model how to read with expression. List on chart paper all the endings children created, and display the list in the classroom. Tell them that you hope they will use similar endings the next time they write a story. The following lesson prepares students to begin their own nonfiction reports, preferably after they have made at least two class books.

Lesson 18: Color-Coding Sentences to Organize Information
<u>Rubric Category:</u> Organization
<u>Writing Goal:</u> Organizing ideas in a logical way

Introduction

Demonstrate a nonfiction, modeled writing about an animal. Tell students that you are writing a **rough draft** and that you are going to write down as many facts as you can. Read your facts aloud as you write them, and think aloud as you remember more information. For example, say, "I also know that cats have whiskers so I am going to write that now before I forget. And I want to make sure to write that cats like to eat fish." Do not attempt to organize your thoughts or to order the list of facts that you write.

Addressing the Writing Goal

After you have written a list of facts, read them to the students. Tell them that you would like to organize your ideas. Tell them that you are going to organize your ideas by using colored markers. Tell the students that by grouping facts together, you are **revising** your rough draft.

Choose one color for each category, and design a "key" for your chapters. For example, for each fact that gives information on what cats eat, use red. For facts that tell about what cats look like, use blue.

Read each fact again, pausing to underline each one with a colored marker.

After all facts have been underlined, tell students that you would like to group the colors together. Explain that by grouping all the red ideas, you will be grouping facts about what cats eat. Remind students that nonfiction books organize information in this way.

On a new piece of chart paper, rewrite your facts. This time, write them in groups based on the information they convey. When all the facts have been organized, write chapter titles above each section. If a group only has two or three facts, refer to a book for additional information on that category.

Final Preparation

Tell the children that they are going to do their own writing about any animal that they choose. Show them the collection of books you have gathered to help them choose their topic. Suggest that they choose an animal they know something about so that when they begin their rough draft, they will have some ideas to write. Tell them that they can look in a book to research more information after they have written a few sentences. Remind them to use crayons to color-code their sentences, just as you did on the chart paper. Before they go and write, ask each child to tell you the animal she has chosen. Ask her to tell you one or two facts about the animal to make sure she has enough knowledge to begin to write.

Individual Conferences

As children are writing, walk around to make sure they are all engaged. After a child has written two or three sentences, allow him to take a book on his animal to do research. Then, when he is ready to color-code his sentences, make sure he has designed a logical system with three or four chapters in mind. After he has underlined all his sentences, ask him to recopy all the information by grouping together the sentences of the same color.

Final Reflection

After children have recopied their rough drafts, work with them individually or in small groups to determine the following:

- Does each chapter have enough information?
- Does the child need to edit any of the words that appear on the word wall?
- Does anything else need to be edited by the teacher?
- Is the writing ready to be published?
- Is the child ready to begin work on nonfiction illustrations/page numbers/a table of contents?

A note about spelling:

Spelling is an integral part of writing and an important skill for children to learn. If, however, children are anxious about spelling every word correctly, they will feel inhibited to write their ideas down on their rough draft for fear of making a mistake. Here we see the importance of the writing process. When we are clear about each step of the writing process and which skills apply to each step, we can be clear with our students. Simply put, we must explain to our students that they should use sound spelling and think about spelling patterns they know when they are working on the rough draft, and that we will check spelling when we edit. And we must do exactly that. While children are still learning the process, we must edit with them as soon as possible, so that they can relieve their anxiety about seeing misspelled words on their page.

We must also examine our teaching of the high-frequency words and our use of the word wall. If children are misspelling high-frequency words, we must address this problem immediately. Children must be responsible for correct spelling of the known high-frequency words on their rough drafts. By mastering these words, children will feel reassured by knowing how to spell them automatically. In turn, they will be reserving their mental energy for addressing unknown words.

Lesson 19: Using Color Coding to Write From Left to Right

Rubric Category: Understanding Conventions

Emergent Writing Goal: Writing from left to right

Teacher Preparation

Chart paper and markers for modeled writing. Draw green circles down the left margin of the chart paper, and draw red circles down the right margin of the chart paper.

Introduction

Tell the children that you are going to write the plans for the day. Explain that it is your turn to think, your turn to write, and their turn to watch and listen. Tell them that they will have a chance to write when you are done.

Addressing the Goal

Before you begin to write, say, "I am going to start my writing next to this green circle because we always begin to write on this side of the paper. Just like on a traffic light, green means 'go,' so I am going to start my writing here." Begin to write the plans. When you get to the red circle, say, "I am going to stop writing here because we always end our line of writing on this side of the page. Just like on a traffic light, red means 'stop' so I am going to stop my writing here." Then say, "I still have more to write, so I am going to go to the next green circle on the next line and keep writing." Continue providing the children with a running commentary of how you are placing your writing on the paper based on the green and red circles.

Final Preparation

Tell the children that you would like them to have a turn to write. Give them paper, pencils, and green and red crayons. Ask them to draw green circles down the left margin and red circles down the right margin, just as you had done. Remind them to begin their writing next to the green circle, stop next to the red circle, and then go back to the next green circle. Make sure each child has an idea, and encourage them to draw a picture before they begin to write.

Individual Conferences

As children begin to write, make sure they are correctly placing their writing on the paper. Do not worry about their letter-sound correlations. Allow them to focus on the goal at hand.

Final Reflection

Gather the children on the rug, and ask them to hold up their work. Give them a minute to look around at each other's writing, and point out how everyone wrote from one side of the page to the other. Remind them to do this every time they write.

Lesson 20: Using the Word Wall and Sound Spelling

<u>Rubric Category:</u> Understanding Conventions

<u>Emergent Writing Goals:</u> Drawing a representational picture, using sound-spelling, using conventional spelling

Teacher Preparation

Chart paper and markets. All materials for writer's workshop ready for the children.

Introduction

Tell the children that after good writers have chosen a topic, they can either draw a picture about their idea before they begin to write or they can start writing and then draw a picture. Explain that drawing and writing are just like speaking because they are ways of sharing ideas with other people.

Addressing the Writing Goals

Share an experience from your life with the children. Draw a picture on the chart paper that shows the story you shared. For example, if you told the children about your trip to the beach, draw a picture of the ocean, the beach, and you sitting on the sand. Tell the children that drawing is a good way to remember all the parts of the story about which they are going to write, and that, if they want to, they can draw before they begin to write.

Note: Many young children formulate their ideas as they draw rather than drawing about what they have previously thought. Drawing is invaluable for the youngest writers because it provides a springboard for their ideas.

After you have finished drawing, tell the children that you are going to write some words to explain the picture. Explain that some words are on the word wall and that you will spell the words just as they appear on the word wall, while other words you will sound out.

Note: Because authenticity and honesty are important to model for children, tell them that even though you know how to spell the words, you will show them how to sound out so that they will know how to sound out the words that they choose.

Begin to write, producing about three sentences. Think aloud about each word you write, asking yourself if the word is on the word wall or if it is a word that you need to sound out.

Final Preparation

Read your sentences aloud. Tell the children that later you will **edit** the words that you did not know how to spell. Explain that when writers are working on a **rough draft**, their most important job is to write down their ideas as quickly as they can before they forget them. Tell them that sounding out is very important because it lets the writer keep writing instead of stopping and worrying about how to spell the word.

Ask the children to raise their hands and to tell you which **strategies** you used to write your **rough draft**. After they have generated all strategies (selecting a topic, drawing a picture, deciding which words to write, using the word wall, and sounding out words), ask them to go and draw and write about the ideas they chose during the last lesson.

Individual Conferences

Conferences can deal with any of the writing goals this lesson addresses. For example, if a child has drawn a picture and has stopped working, you might say, "What an interesting picture. Tell me about it." After the child has explained the picture, you might reiterate what the child said by creating a sentence that she can write. For example, you could say, "Your idea is 'I like to swim.' What is the first word you are going to write? Where can you look to see how to write that word?"

In another example, you might come across a child who has written a couple of sentences and then stopped. You could say, "I would love to read your writing! Is that OK?" After reading, you might say, "I can't wait to read the next sentence you are going to write. Maybe you'll decide to tell us what your cat looks like. I'll be back in a minute to see what you have written."

Final Reflection

After proceeding through the regular sharing procedure, ask the following questions:

- "Who drew a picture first and then wrote?"
- "Who wrote first?"
- "Who wrote words that are on the word wall?"
- "Who wrote the word 'the'? (Go on to call out a few more words.)
- "Who sounded out words?"

Lesson 21: Writing High-Frequency Words
Rubric Category: Understanding Conventions (Spelling)
Emergent Goal: Learning conventional spelling

Teacher Preparation

Select a big book that contains some of the high-frequency words that children need to learn. Have pencils and paper ready for the children to use.

Introduction

First, read the book aloud so that the children can enjoy the story. Read the book a second and third time as a shared reading, encouraging the children to read along with you.

Note: The initial three readings of the big book give children enough familiarity with the book so that they are able to focus on the following lesson without being distracted by other features of the book.

Addressing the Writing Goal

- Tell the children that the word "in," for example, appears many times in the book.
- Write the word "in" on chart paper as the children watch.
- Ask the children to "write" the word in the air and to spell it as they "write."
- Ask how many letters are in the word.

Final Preparation

- Distribute pencils and paper.
- Tell the children that you will read the book to them again, and that they should write the word "in" each time they hear you read it.
- Emphasize the word "in" each time you read it, and pause to give the children time to write it.
- Count how many times the word "in" appears in the book.
- Ask the children to count how many times they wrote the word on their paper and to make sure their number is correct.
- Write the word on an index card and put it on the word wall.
- Tell the children that they are to write the word correctly whenever they write it.

Individual Conferences

Quietly praise each child who uses the high-frequency word(s) taught from the big book.

Final Reflection

After the children have held up their work, ask the following questions:

- "Who wrote the word 'in'?"
- "Who spelled the word just the way it is spelled on the word wall?"

Lesson 22: *Writing Dictated Sentences*
__Rubric Category:__ Understanding Conventions (Spelling)
__Emergent Writing Goal:__ Using Conventional Spelling

Teacher Preparation

Paper, pencils, and individual word lists for children to use as they write (See page 13). Write the following list of sentences, which are comprised of only high-frequency words.

Look up./I look up./We look up./I go up./I am up./I am here./I see it./I am in./I like to come here./I like to go here./I am in here./This is it./I come here./We come here./Come to me./Look at it./Here I go./Look at me./I go in./I like this./I see this./Look here./Come see this./

Introduction

Tell the children that some words they will see in books and write very often. Explain to them that they need to learn how to write these words so that they do not have to worry about sounding them out.

Addressing the Writing Goal

Give each child a "personal word wall" that has the high frequency words arranged in alphabetical order. (See list on page 13)

Dictate one sentence at a time, reading slowly, and making sure each child is keeping up. Help the children locate each word on their list if they need a reference, but do not spell the words aloud for them.

Lesson 23: *Using the Word Wall to Spell High-Frequency Words*
__Rubric Category:__ Understanding Conventions (Spelling)
__Writing Goal:__ Correctly spelling the high-frequency words that are on the word wall

Teacher Preparation

Select writing from a child who has correctly spelled words from the word wall. Ask the child for permission to show his revision to the class. Make a copy of the child's writing to show on an overhead projector.

Introduction

Tell the children that one of their friends has agreed to show his writing to them. Show the writing on the overhead. Read it aloud. Praise the writing, and ask if anyone has something nice to say to the writer.

Addressing the Writing Goal

Ask if anyone sees a word from the word wall on the child's paper. Ask the writer to find the word and underline it. Then ask the writer to read the word and then spell it. Then ask the child to look at the word wall and spell the word as it appears there. Ask the children if the word is spell correctly. Tell the children that every time they write a word that appears on the word wall, they must spell it correctly. When the child has finished writing, read the sentences aloud. Praise the writer for doing a good job and for sharing his work. Explain that correct spelling helps the audience read the words. Tell the children that we call this part of the writing process "editing."

Final Preparation

Ask the children to choose a piece they have already revised and to put a line under all the words that come from the word wall. Ask them to make sure the words are spelled correctly. Tell them again that this is called **editing**.

Individual Conferences

Walk around the room, maintaining a quiet working environment. Offer praise and encouragement and use a quiet whisper.

Note: If children are expected to use the word wall, be sure they can see it easily. The words must be large and clearly written.

Final Reflection

Gather the children on the rug in a circle. Ask them to hold up their work so that their friends can see them. Ask children to raise their hands if they:

- Underlined words that appear on the word wall.
- Checked that the words were spelled correctly.

Ask children to spell one of the words they wrote.

Note: Ultimately, children should correctly spell the words from the word wall when they write their rough drafts and should not have to wait to correct them when they edit. Editing will be used to correct punctuation, capitalization, and spelling words that require help from the teacher.

Lesson 24: *Correcting Errors in the Class Plans*

Rubric Category: Understanding Conventions

Writing Goals: Spelling high-frequency words, using periods, using capitals at the beginning of sentences

Teacher Preparation

Prepare the daily plans to write on chart paper. Think about how to write them in a narrative form, as a paragraph, rather than as a list or as a schedule. This lesson should be done over several days before children are asked to edit their own papers.

Introduction

Tell the children that you are going to write the daily plans and that you are going to make some mistakes. Tell them to listen and watch quietly. Tell them that when you are finished, they will help you edit.

As you write, think aloud about when to use periods, capitals, and about how to spell the words on the word wall. For example, say, "This is the beginning of a sentence, and so I will use a capital letter"; "Here is the end of my sentence, and so I will use a period"; or "This word is on the word wall, and so I will check how to spell it."

Omit some of the punctuation and capital letters and spell some of the words incorrectly. Do not say anything about the errors.

Addressing the Writing Goal

When you are finished, ask the children if they see mistakes. Ask several to come up to the chart paper and edit your mistakes with a magic marker.

Final Preparation

Tell the children that they will be editing some of their own writing. Ask them to choose a revision from a previous day and to edit punctuation, capitalization, and spelling mistakes.

Note: Tell the children that your mistakes are deliberate. Authenticity in teaching promotes honest and open interactions with children. Use the word, **edit,** so that they learn the term and its meaning.

Individual Conferences

- Walk around the room, maintaining a quiet working environment.
- Offer praise and encouragement, and use a quiet whisper.
- Point out places on their paper where children may need a capital letter or a period.

Note: Children will need a lot of support with editing. They should not be expected to edit thoroughly without help. They should learn, however, how and why to edit.

Final Reflection

Gather the children on the rug in a circle. Ask them to hold up their work so that their friends can see it. Ask children to raise their hands if they:

- Underlined words that appear on the word wall.
- Checked that the words were spelled correctly.
- Added periods.
- Added capital letters.

Ask children to spell one of the words they wrote.

Note: Ultimately, children should correctly spell the words from the word wall as they write their rough draft and not wait to correct them when they edit. Editing will be used to correct punctuation, capitalization, and spelling words that require help from the teacher.

Lesson 25: Using a Traditional Tale to Teach Possessive Nouns
Rubric Category: Understanding Conventions (Punctuation)
Writing Goal: Using an apostrophe with a possessive noun

Teacher Preparation

Get a copy of *The Three Bears*. Have chart paper, markers, and all materials for writer's workshop ready.

Introduction

Read *The Three Bears* as a read-aloud. Before a second reading of the story, tell students that when writers want to show to whom things belong, they put the sound "s" at the end of the character's name. Give them examples, such as "Mama Bear's chair" and "Baby Bear's bed." Tell students to listen for the times that the author uses this strategy and to give a thumbs-up each time they hear it.

Addressing the Writing Goal

On chart paper, show students how to write an apostrophe and the letter "s" to show that something belongs to a character. Explain that if writers do not use the apostrophe, the word means that there is more than one. For example, show them that the words "baby bears" means that there are many baby bears, but that the words Baby Bear's" means that something belongs to him. Ask students to come up to the chart paper and practice writing one of the character's names with an apostrophe and an "s" after the name.

Final Preparation

Tell students that they are going to write about *The Three Bears* and that you want them to tell about the time Goldilocks used all of the bear family's things. For example, suggest that they write about Goldilocks eating Baby Bear's porridge. Allow students an opportunity to rehearse orally what they are going to write, being sure to use an apostrophe and an "s" to tell to whom things belong.

Individual Conferencing

While students are writing, quietly confer with individuals to make sure they remember their ideas and to use an apostrophe and an "s" at the end of the characters' names.

Final Reflection

Gather students on the rug in a circle. Ask them to hold up their letters so that their classmates can see them. Ask students to raise their hands if they:

- Wrote about the three bears.
- Used an apostrophe and an "s."

Applaud for each other.

Lesson 26: Using a Traditional Tale to Teach Quotation Marks
Rubric Category: Understanding Conventions (Punctuation)
Writing Goal: Using quotation marks for dialogue

Teacher Preparation

The Three Bears, chart paper, markers, and all materials for writer's workshop.

Introduction

Reread *The Three Bears*. Before reading, remind students about the part when the bears came home to find that someone had been using their things. Ask students if they remember what the bears said and allow them opportunity to quote them (For example, "Someone's been eating my porridge!") Tell students that you would like them to read along during the parts when the bears speak. Practice a few lines with them.

Addressing the Writing Goal

Tell students that when authors write, they use symbols called "quotation marks" to show readers that a character is speaking. Show students quotation marks in the text of *The Three Bears*. On chart paper, write some of the bears' quotes but leave out the quotation marks. Ask students to come up and add the quotation marks.

Final Preparation

Tell students that you would like them to write about the story and to tell about the part when the bears came home. Tell them to make sure to write what the bears said. Allow them to rehearse orally what they are going to write.

Individual Conferencing

While students are writing, quietly confer with individuals about their ideas. Make sure they are using quotation marks.

Final Reflection

Gather students on the rug in a circle. Ask them to hold up their letters so that their classmates can see them. Ask students to raise their hands if they:

- Wrote about the three bears coming home.
- Used quotation marks.

Applaud for each other.

Lesson 27: Using a Traditional Tale to Teach the Past Tense of Some Irregular Verbs

Rubric Category: Understanding Conventions (Grammar)

Writing Goal: Maintaining past, present, or future tense

Teacher Preparation

The Gingerbread Man, chart paper.

Introduction

Read *The Gingerbread Man* as a read-aloud. Before you read it again, tell students that when writers want to tell about something that happened, they have to change the word that tells about what happened. For example, tell them that the word "run" changes to "ran" when it talks about what the gingerbread man and the other characters already did. During the second reading, tell students to give a thumbs-up each time they hear the word "ran."

Addressing the Writing Goal

On chart paper, show students how to write the word "run" and the word "ran." Underline the middle vowel to show them how the word changes. Ask several students to come up to the chart paper and practice writing the word "run." Add to their word with the remainder of the text: "**Run, run,** as fast as you can." Then ask students to come up and write the word "ran." Add to their word with the remainder of the text: "The Gingerbread Man **ran** on and on, past houses and trees."

Final Preparation

Tell students that they are going to write about the Gingerbread Man. They should write using the words "run" and "ran." Allow students an opportunity to rehearse orally what they are going to write, being sure to use the words "run" and "ran."

Individual Conferencing

While students are writing, quietly confer with individuals to make sure they remember their ideas and to use the words "run" and "ran."

Final Reflection

Gather students on the rug in a circle. Ask them to hold up their letters so that their classmates can see them. Ask students to raise their hands if they:

- Wrote the word "run."
- Wrote the word "ran."

Applaud for each other.

Lesson 28: Preparing a Child's Writing for Publishing

Rubric Category: Understanding Conventions

Writing Goals: Using correct spelling, punctuation, capitalization

Teacher Preparation

This lesson requires that the child has taken a piece of writing through the previous steps of the writing process (rough draft, revising, and editing). Ask the child to bring her edited writing to you with a pencil and a clean sheet of paper. Make sure you have access to a computer.

Introduction

After the child reads her piece to you, ask her if she has finished editing. If necessary, complete the editing process while the child watches.

Addressing the Writing Goal

Explain that writers must make sure their work is ready for other people to read before the work is published. Point out that spelling, punctuation, and capitalization are important parts of good writing because they help the audience read correctly.

Look at the handwriting. Decide if the child should spend some time recopying two or three sentences or if the handwriting looks acceptable. Explain your decision to the child. If the child needs to recopy, have her use a clean sheet of paper and help her focus on correct letter formation.

Note: Recopying addresses the need for handwriting practice. Children should not have to put their edited work into a perfectly neat final form if the original handwriting is acceptable. If recopying is recommended, it is important to make sure that the child does not become frustrated. Adjust the number of sentences to be recopied accordingly.

Individual Conferences

After the writing is in its final form, sit with the child at the computer and type out the piece of writing. If the child is an emergent reader, put one sentence on each page so that he will have an easier time reading his book. For more advanced readers, you might want more text on each page, but keep in mind that the child will be illustrating each page and may not know what to draw if there are too many ideas on a single page.

Ask the child for a title, offering suggestions if necessary. Under the title, type, "Written and Illustrated by (child's name)."

- Choose a font that is fairly large. Space twice between words. The text should be clear and easy for children to read.
- Give the child the pages of his/her book.
- Ask the child to read the writing to you, offering help if needed.
- Explain that each page needs an illustration, and that each illustration should show what the words tell.
- Use a book-binding machine if available, or a stapler, to finish the book.

Final Reflection

Celebrate the child's achievement by inviting her to read the book in the "Author's Chair." Display the published books in the classroom under a sign that says "Published Work by Local Authors," alongside books written by favorite authors. Invite parents to author parties in the classroom to listen to the children read their books. Children can visit other classrooms to read their books, or they can invite other classes to their rooms to see their published work. For a more elaborate and exciting event, schools can hold a "Young Authors' Conference," during which every child in the school presents a published book to a small group of children, teachers, and parents.

The Importance of Publishing

Teaching the entire writing process necessarily involves publishing children's writing. While the primary purpose of the writing process is to teach all the skills of writing in a sequential way, honoring the final published product is a very important aspect of writing instruction. As children learn that the final step in the writing process is to publish, they soon realize that the real purpose of writing is to share their written ideas with others. They begin to understand that we write so that others may read what we have written.

Young children should not publish every rough draft they begin, but they should be expected to publish a few books of their choosing during the course of the year. The precise number depends on each teacher and each child. Publishing increases motivation to write and gives students an authentic reason to put effort into their writing. Knowing that someone is going to read his words encourages a child to write well. It helps children understand the concept of writing to an audience. Learning becomes more purposeful and less arbitrary. Children thrive when they feel that they are making important contributions to others.

Because of the significance of the publishing step, publishing individual books starting in kindergarten is important. The motivation that publishing creates cannot be overestimated. The more children write and realize that others are reading their ideas, the more they want to write. This is our goal.

It is important for kindergartners to experience independent writing. As they move through the writing process, we should offer a great deal of support. We may help them do their "sound-spelling" and to isolate each word in their sentence, but they are holding the pencil and creating a rough draft. We help them read their rough draft and suggest they add a word or a sentence, but they are holding the pencil, making the changes, and creating a revision. We may also help them check for a period at the end of their sentence, but, again, they are doing the writing and, in this case, the editing. Once they have edited, we can help them with a final edit, explaining that all authors need to spell words the same way when they publish books.

There is no criticism, shaming, or discouraging. The children simply learn that all writers need help with editing, and that the result is a published book. After they have seen their book printed on the computer with their name on the cover, the enthusiasm stays with them as they begin their next rough draft.

Conclusion

The face of American education continues to change. Larger numbers of immigrant children greet us each year. Children from families of all types impel us to continue to examine our beliefs and adjust our teaching practices. As these student populations increase in our classrooms, so does our responsibility to educate them.

In my experience, this task has been a joyous one. While many of my students are poor and/or just learning English, I can also describe them as bright, enthusiastic, brave, and eager to embrace knowledge. I am humbled by the way my young students straddle two cultures and two languages each day as they leave their homes and come to school. Their openness and their courage have touched me, and I feel privileged to teach them.

I offer the following guidelines developed during my journey as a teacher of writing. May they serve you well.

- Insist that the children try to talk. Do not push, but over time, do not accept passivity!
- Watch the faces and the expression in their eyes. Are they engaged? Are they at ease?
- Be acquainted with, and be able to describe, the unique life of each child.
- Make yourself familiar with wonderful children's literature—both fiction and nonfiction—and use it to enrich the lives of your students.
- Understand the developmental stages of writing.
- Be able to identify the level of good writing characteristics shown in the writing of each child.
- Learn to select and model three or four specific skills at a time for each child that will help him move to the next level.
- Make sure that each lesson matches the skills you are trying to teach.

Above all, remember that young writers are children first. Carry the knowledge that with our guidance they are progressing along a developmental path; that every classroom is a community; and that all children deserve to feel valued, nurtured, and happy. Only then will they be ready to learn what we can teach them.

Annotated Bibliography For Extending Children's Ideas

* Denotes nonfiction titles

Adoption

Joosse, Barbara M. *Mama, Do You Love Me?*

A young Inuit girl tests her mother's love by asking, "What if..." to various scenarios in which she does something wrong.

Pellegrini, Nina. *Families Are Different*

A little girl is adopted from Korea. She explains that she and her adopted sister look different from their parents and that she used to feel sad and angry about it. After her mother tells her that there are many different kinds of families, and that a family's love is the most important thing, she feels very happy.

Animals

*French, Vivian. *Growing Frogs*

The lifecycle of a frog is explained, as told in a narrative by a little girl who gathers frog eggs and watches them hatch and grow. It includes bright, colorful illustrations, with captions that provide additional information.

*Gibbons, Gail. *Horses!*

The history, the types, the parts, and the care of horses are explained. Rich, detailed drawings have labels and captions, and include cross-sections and enlarged sections. (Excellent model for children to follow as they learn nonfiction illustrating.)

*Hansard, Peter. *A Field Full of Horses*

A beautiful narrative that is richly embedded with facts. The engaging text, written in first person, invites readers to respond to questions and actively learn about horses. The wonderful illustrations have captions and labels, providing additional facts. (Excellent model for children to follow as they learn nonfiction illustrating.)

*Jenkins, Martin. *Chameleons Are Cool*

> Rich, colorful illustrations are accompanied by captions and humorous text. Includes an index.

*Jenkins, Martin. *The Emperor's Egg*

> Humorous, engaging text, teaches about Emperor penguins. It includes captions, labels, enlarged words to emphasize exclamations, and an index.

Creativity

Carle, Eric. *The Very Busy Spider*

> As a spider spins her web, various farm animals try to interfere with her efforts. The spider persists and creates a beautiful, intricate, and useful web.

DePaola, Tomie. *The Art Lesson*

> Tomie is a little boy who loves to draw. His family encourages and celebrates his drawings and puts them up around the house. When Tomie gets to first grade, his teachers only gives him one sheet of paper, a few crayons, and expect him to copy other pictures. Tomie becomes discouraged and frustrated, until his art teacher understands his feelings and begins to nurture his artistic talent.

Gilman, Phoebe. *Something from Nothing*

> A Jewish folktale that tells about a special old blanket that continuously is transformed into something new as it becomes too old and shabby for its previous use.

Haring, Keith. *Big*

> Wonderful, amusing illustrations by artist Keith Haring show children dressing up in enormous clothing. The text consists of simple phrases, labeling the pictures with synonyms for the word, "big."

Taback, Simms. *Joseph Had a Little Overcoat*

> A man has a beloved coat that gets haggard, and so he keeps making it into new things. However, he never stops enjoying it. Eventually, the coat is only a button, which the man loses causing him to be extremely sad. Nonetheless, he makes a book about his coat to show that you can always make something out of nothing.

Fathers

Isadora, Rachel. *At the Crossroads*

> A group of children living in a squatter camp in South Africa awaits

the return of their fathers who have been away for ten months working in the mines. They sing and dance as they wait, but night falls and they do not see their fathers. They wait all night until the joyous reunion.

Feelings

Bang, Molly. *When Sophie Gets Angry—Really, Really Angry*
> Sophie feels very angry. She leaves the house and goes on an imaginary journey to feel better. She comes back home in a much better mood.

Curtis, Jamie Lee. *Today I Feel Silly & Other Moods That Make My Day*
> Through amusing rhymes and engaging illustrations, we read about a child's range of emotions and escapades.

Henkes, Kevin. *Lilly's Purple Plastic Purse*
> Lilly loves school and especially adores her teacher. After he takes away her purse because she is disrupting the class, she feels very angry and writes him a mean, insulting note. Later, she finds a kind note from her teacher in her purse, and she feels terrible. She apologizes with her own letter and picture expressing her remorse.

Sendak, Maurice. *Where the Wild Things Are*
> When Max acts in a wild and oppositional way towards his mother, she sends him to his room without dinner. Max imagines that he travels across the ocean to a land of wild creatures, where he becomes king. After a while, he decides to return home, and finds himself back in his room where his supper is waiting.

Viorst, Judith. *Alexander and the Terrible, Horrible, No Good, Very Bad Day*
> Alexander has an upsetting day, where everything goes wrong!

Wood, Audrey. *Quick as a Cricket*
> A child expresses feelings through the characteristics of animals.

Freedom

*Demi. *Gandhi*
> A biography of Mahatma Gandhi, who led the nonviolent civil rights movement in India and the liberation of India from Great Britain.

Hopkinson, Deborah. *Under the Quilt of Night*
> A dramatic account of a child's escape from slavery along the Underground Railroad. Beautiful. Moving illustrations and rich imagery in the language.

*Krull, Kathleen. *Harvesting Hope*
> This is a biography of Cesar Chavez, who became a leader in the fight for rights for farm workers.

*Rappaport, Doreen. *Martin's Big Words: The Life of Dr. Martin Luther King, Jr.*
> Dramatic, powerful illustrations depict the life of Martin Luther King and the Civil Rights Movement. Famous quotes from his sermons and speeches accompany the text.

Ringgold, Faith. *Aunt Harriet's Underground Railroad in the Sky*
> A little girl imagines that she is escaping slavery and traveling on the underground railway with Harriet Tubman.

Friendship

Bruchac, Joseph. *The First Strawberries: A Cherokee Story*
> A gentle Cherokee legend, retold by Bruchac, tells of a fight between a husband and wife. The simple text and beautiful illustrations depict how the sun created strawberries, which, in turn, helped to restore respect and friendship between the man and woman.

Cannon, Janell. *Stellaluna*
> A baby bat loses her mother and is adopted by a family of birds. The bat and the birds become dear friends, in spite of their differences.

Fox, Mem. *Wilfrid Gordon McDonald Partridge*
> A little boy lives next door to a retirement home. He visits often and has a special friend there. He learns that she has lost her memory, and so he asks each of the other elderly people to explain to him what a memory is. He takes their explanations, such as "something that makes you laugh," and matches each one to a special object that he brings to his friend to help her remember.

Heine, Helme. *Friends*
> Three friends—a pig, a rooster, and a mouse—spend all day playing together and sharing adventures. They solve problems so that each of them feels happy. However, at bedtime, they learn that they must each return to their homes to sleep comfortably. They sadly part, but they are happy once again when they dream about each other.

Jones, Rebecca C. *Matthew and Tilly*
> Matthew and Tilly are friends who live in next-door apartments.

One day they have a fight, insult each other, and stop playing together. They become lonely playing alone, and so they apologize to each other and play together again.

Marshall, James. *George and Martha*

A collection of short stories about two friends. The stories depict their conversations and adventures. The stories show how friends offer reassurance and encouragement to each other and demonstrate the importance of honesty.

Rylant, Cynthia. *The Old Woman Who Named Things*

An old woman has outlived all her friends. To keep from feeling lonely, she names all the important objects in her life. When a stray puppy appears, she rediscovers the importance of companionship.

Steig, William. *Amos and Boris*

Amos, the mouse, falls off his boat and into the ocean. Boris, the whale, rescues him. They become dear friends, sharing adventures and stories. When Boris returns Amos to land, they vow their eternal friendship to each other, and Amos promises to repay Boris for his help. Years later, he eventually does by saving Boris' life. They realize their goodbye may be a final farewell, but they also realize that they will be friends forever.

Waber, Bernard. *Lyle, Lyle, Crocodile*

Lyle is a crocodile who lives with the Primm family in New York. He is friendly and playful and lives happily with the family. Their neighbor, Mr. Grumps, wants to get rid of Lyle because he scares Mr. Grump's cat, Loretta. After being sent to the zoo by Mr. Grumps, Lyle eventually escapes. He rescues Loretta and Mr. Grumps from their burning home and is finally welcomed by his neighbor.

Wood, Audrey. *The Napping House*

A child, a grandmother, and an amusing menagerie of animals pile on top of each other as they sleep.

Grandparents

Bunting, Eve. *The Wall*

A father and son visit the Vietnam Memorial to look for the name of the boy's grandfather. The boy sees a grandfather and grandson walking past him, and feels sad that he cannot be with his own grandfather.

DePaola, Tomie. *Now One Foot, Now the Other*

A young boy sees his grandfather recover from a stroke and cares for him the way the grandfather used to nurture the boy.

Fox, Mem. *Possum Magic*

Grandmother Possum turns Hush invisible, which allows him to do all sorts of fun and different activities. However, later on he wants to become visible again and together Hush and Grandmother go all over Australia together eating different types of food until they find the food that makes Hush visible again.

Individuality

Carle, Eric. *A House for Hermit Crab*

After a hermit crab moves into a new shell, he decorates it with the help of other sea creatures.

DePaola, Tomie. *Oliver Button Is A Sissy*

Oliver Button is a little boy who loves to sing, dance, and dress up. His parents send him to dance classes. The other boys tease Oliver and call him a sissy. However, Oliver continues to dance and even performs in the talent show. After his performance, the other children stop teasing him.

Leaf, Munro. *The Story of Ferdinand*

Ferdinand the bull loves to sit and smell the flowers and does not run and play with the other bulls. He continues this behavior every day until the day the men from the bullfight come in search of the meanest and strongest bull. Strangely, that same afternoon Ferdinand is stung by a bee and gets very angry; thus, the men pick him for the bullfight. Ferdinand goes to the bullfight, but he just sits there and smells the flowers in the women's hair who are sitting in the audience. Therefore, they cannot have a bullfight and take Ferdinand home.

Lionni, Leo. *Fish Is Fish*

A little fish wants to know what life is like outside the water. With the help of a friend, he learns to accept himself for who he is—a fish.

Wells, Rosemary. *Yoko*

Yoko's mother makes her favorite school lunch for her, sushi. The other children make fun of Yoko's food. The teacher organizes an international food day to try to help Yoko with her problem. Still, the other children refuse to try the sushi. Finally, Timothy tries Yoko's food and loves it. They become good friends.

Leaving Home

Bresnick-Perry, Roslyn. *Leaving for America*

> A little girl lives with her mother in a small Jewish town in Russia. Her father is in America, working to earn money so that he can send for his family. As they prepare to join him, the little girl describes events and people in her life.

Bunting, Eve. *Going Home*

> A family of Mexican migrant workers returns to Mexico to celebrate Christmas. The children see how happy their parents are to be home and realize the sacrifice they have made by leaving Mexico in order to earn money in the United States.

Bunting, Eve. *How Many Days to America? A Thanksgiving Story*

> A family escapes war in their Caribbean homeland and flees to America. The journey is grueling and dangerous, but the children's father comforts them with a song and they continue. Eventually, after many hurdles, they reach America. The day is Thanksgiving, and they are greeted with a feast and with the true meaning of Thanksgiving.

Polacco, Patricia. *The Keeping Quilt*

> Russian-Jewish immigrants create a quilt that depicts their lives in Russia. The quilt is passed down from mother to daughter across generations. The story shows how the family members maintained their heritage and identity as they became Americanized.

Williams, Karen Lynn. *When Africa Was Home*

> A young American boy lives with his parents in rural Africa. He has friends and loves his life outdoors under the African sun. When they return to America, he is very sad and misses Africa.

Mothers/Love

Fox, Mem. *Koala Lou*

> A little koala adores her mother who adores her in return. After many brothers and sisters are born, however, Koala Lou feels neglected and misses her mother's attention. She decides to enter a race so that

when she wins, her mother will once again be proud of her and show her affection. She does not win, but she learns that her mother never stopped loving her, and Koala Lou feels comforted again.

Fox, Mem. *Time for Bed*

Animal parents gently speak to their babies at bedtime.

Freeman, Marcia S. *The Gift.*

Sonja and her family suffer tribulations when they emigrate from Norway to the American prairie. Her mother's joyful singing sustains the family during this time, but soon her mother's songs are silenced by loneliness. Sonja finds a way to bring back the songs and her family's hope and happiness.

Joosse, Barbara M. *Mama, Do You Love Me?*

A young Inuit girl tests her mother's love by asking "What if..." to various scenarios in which she does something wrong.

Polacco, Patricia. *Betty Doll* (Not appropriate for children under seven years old)

A young girl tells about her doll that has always given her comfort. The book tells about a mother and daughter's trials, including their house burning, fighting cancer, a divorce, and leaving home.

Persistence/Courage

*Atkin, S. Beth. *Voices from the Fields: Children of Migrant Farmworkers Tell Their Stories* (Nonfiction; second grade and older)

Migrant children share their hopes, dreams, fears, and sorrows, as they write about their lives.

Brett, Jan. *Daisy Comes Home*

Set in China, the story tells of how a timid pet hen became lost, overcame dangerous threats, and learned to be courageous. The illustrations depict life in modern-day China, and are rich, detailed, and colorful.

Burton, Virginia Lee. *Mike Mulligan And His Steam Shovel*

Mike Mulligan and his steam shovel, Mary Anne, have worked together for years building cities. When bulldozers that are more modern are invented, they become obsolete. Therefore, they leave the city and head for the countryside. There, they offer to dig the cellar for the new town hall and promise to finish by sundown. With the encouragement of the townspeople, they succeed. Because they have no way to get out, they live in the cellar where Mary Anne becomes the furnace and Mike becomes the janitor.

*Coles, Robert. *The Story of Ruby Bridges*
   A biography of courageous first grader Ruby Bridges who withstood the hatred of racism. The only black child to attend an all white school in New Orleans in 1960, Ruby was accompanied by federal marshals to ensure her safety.

Freeman, Don. *Norman the Doorman*
   Norman is a mouse who lives under an art museum. He maintains his own art gallery for mice and works as the doorman there. Norman is also an artist and loves to create. When he learns about an art competition, he decides to enter. He wins the competition, as well as the admiration of the judges, and achieves his wish to tour the gallery without fear of being caught.

*Jordan, Deloris. *Salt in His Shoes*
   Written by Jordan's mother, this picture-book biography of a basketball legend humorously and lovingly conveys his persistence and determination to be successful.

*Krull, Kathleen. *Lives of Extraordinary Women*
   The author describes the biographies of twenty women from around the world, including personal, humorous, and shocking facts.

Lionni, Leo. *Swimmy*
   After a small fish, along with his brothers and sisters, escapes from being eaten, he travels the ocean and discovers its beauty and magic. He finds another school of fish, who are hiding in fear of being eaten, too. Swimmy convinces them that they cannot live in fear and shows them how to work together to overcome their fears.

Ringgold, Faith. *Tar Beach*
   A young girl imagines that she is flying over New York City and thinks of ways to create a better life for her family.

Steig, William. *Brave Irene*
   A little girl helps her sick mother by braving the snow to take a dress made by her mother to the duchess. She struggles through the storm, losing the dress along the way, until she reaches the home of the duchess, just in time for the ball. All turns out well, and Irene proves to be a very brave and loving child.

Steig, William. *Dr. DeSoto*

> A mouse dentist and his wife treat a conniving wolf with a toothache. In the end, they prove their own ingenuity.

St. George, Judith. *So You Want to Be President?*

> Fun facts, cartoon drawings, and familiar presidents fill this book, which explains that presidents are just people with good and bad qualities.

Self-esteem

Carlson, Nancy. *I Like Me*

> A little pig tells about how much she loves herself.

Hoffman, Mary and Binch, Caroline. *Amazing Grace*

> Grace loves listening to stories and acting them out. When her teacher announces that the class will be performing "Peter Pan," Grace announces that she wants to be Peter Pan. The other children tell her she cannot because she is a girl and because she is black. With her grandmother's help, Grace learns that she can do whatever she wants to do if she puts her mind to it.

Siblings/New Baby

Keats, Ezra Jack. *Peter's Chair*

> Peter feels angry and jealous as he sees his new baby sister being given all his baby furniture. He decides to run away with his dog and some of his baby things. When he realizes that he is too big for his baby chair, he suggests to his father that they paint it pink for his sister and give it to her.

Polacco, Patricia. *My Rotten Redheaded Older Brother*

> An older brother is always able to do things better than his younger sister, which frustrates her. The girl has an accident and her brother saves her.

Whybrow, Ian. *A Baby for Grace*

> Grace feels ignored after her brother is born. She hears a lot of "no" from the adults around her. Finally, her father gives her the attention and the "yes" to make her feel loved again.

References

Avery, Carol. (1993). . . . *And with a Light Touch.* Portsmouth, NH: Heinemann.

Calkins, Lucy McCormick. (1986). *The Art of Teaching Writing.* Portsmouth, New Hampshire: Heinemann Educational Books.

Clay, Marie M. (1975). *What Did I Write? Beginning Writing Behaviour.* Portsmouth, NH: Heinemann Educational.

Clay, Marie M. (1991). *Becoming Literate.* Portsmouth, NH: Heinemann.

Cummins, Jim. (1979) Cognitive/academic language proficiency, linguistic interdependence, the optimum age question and some other matters. Working Papers on Bilingualism, No. 19, 121-129.

Cunningham, Patricia. (1995). *Phonics They Use.* New York: Harper Collins College Publishers.

Duckworth, Eleanor. (1987). *"The Having of Wonderful Ideas" and Other Essays on Teaching and Learning.* New York: Teachers College Press.

Freeman, Marcia S. (1998). *Teaching the Youngest Writers.* Gainesville, FL: Maupin House Publishing, Inc.

Ginott, Haim G. (1997). *Between Teacher and Child.* New York: Simon and Schuster.

Graves, Donald H. (1983). *Writing: Teachers and Children at Work.* Portsmouth, New Hampshire: Heinemann Educational Books.

Greg and Steve. "*Kidding Around.*" Bloomfield Hills, MI: Songs for Teaching.

Hodgkinson, Harold L. (2003). *Leaving Too Many Children Behind.* Washington, D.C.: The Institute for Educational Leadership.

Murray, Donald M. (1982). *Learning by Teaching.* Upper Montclair, NJ: Boynton/Cook Publishers.

National Writing Project & Carl Nagin. (2003). *Because Writing Matters.* San Francisco, CA: Jossey-Bass.

Nieto, Sonia. (2002). *Language, Culture, and Teaching. Critical Perspectives for a New Century.* Mahwah, New Jersey: Lawrence Erlbaum Associates, Publishers.

Snowball, Diane and Bolton, Faye. (1999). *Spelling K-8.* York, Maine: Stenhouse Publishers.

Taberski, Sharon. (2000). *On Solid Ground.* Portsmouth, NH: Heinemann.

Tabors, Patton O. (1997). *One Child, Two Languages.* Baltimore, MD: Paul H. Brookes Publishing Co.

Index